My Boob Tried To Kill Me!

A Cancer Survivors Journal

by
Lisa Jane Holman

CONTENTS

DEDICATION

To all of the people who have supported me through this journey, I cannot thank you enough. There are so many of you that I believe deserve a special mention;

My best friend, soulmate and wonderful husband, Simon. Without whom, I would not have had the strength to continue.

My amazing daughter, Rachael, who has no idea how her love and support helped me through.

Also, thanks to her wonderful partner, Jamie, for supporting me and being there for Rachael through everything.

Her friend Roxy also deserves a special mention, as she exceeded what would have been expected of her.

My resilient son, Harrison. Despite everything, his humour and compassion shone through.

My Dad, Mum, sister Joanne, and step-mum Sue, despite being miles away, I felt your love and support through our weekly phone calls and text messages.

The people below also deserve a special mention. My friends are the family I was lucky enough to choose for myself, and they will always have a special place in my heart. When most would have run away and buried their heads in the sand, they chose to stand firm and have my back, showing me what true friendship looks like;

Narva, Tash, Karin, The Williams Family, The Finch Family, Rachel H, Sabrina, Sarah, Steve and Marie, Clare, Tracey, Leeann, Selena, Dr Kate, Bev T, Bev S, Kev, Lorien, Alan, Craig, Gemma, Rachael S, Marianne, Julie and Howard.
In your own individual way, you helped me through, even though you didn't realise it at the time.

Thank you to my proofreaders: Sue, Rachel, Sarah and Lorien. After writing these words, I could not reread them.

Last but not least, Alex Lowe, the comedic genius behind the character that is the one and only Clinton Baptiste. Your show in Frome in 2024 made me laugh so hard that my stomach hurt, and I felt alive for the first time in quite a while. You also showed people that cancer patients are still the same and that they still want the same things. So, you shouldn't be afraid to treat them exactly as you always have, regardless of the trials or tribulations they may be encountering.

FOREWORD

I am a private person and not one to air my dirty laundry in public. Therefore, it is very hard to think of a complete stranger thumbing through these pages, the pages of my innermost thoughts and feelings that detail the most challenging fight I have ever faced in my forty-seven years. But, I hope that by laying my life bare for all to see, it will help at least one person who is having to face this awful disease, possibly alone, feel supported and loved. To feel like you have suddenly become a leper because you have an illness and your friends ignore you isn't great, and to do this when you are facing one of the hardest challenges you may ever encounter is a double whammy.

We all have some friends that we consider our ride-or-die friends. Pre-diagnosis, I believed I had a few and could rely on them. I felt that they would have my back, as I would also have had theirs, and I would have been there for them regardless of how long they needed or wanted me.

After my diagnosis, most of my friends, bar the few mentioned by name within these pages, disappeared. They rarely made contact; I only heard from them if I messaged them first, asking how they were. Mostly, the messages from those friends who did respond revolved around their own lives, with little thought or enquiry as to how I was getting along.

Whilst I know our fight or flight response is an automatic psychological reaction to various traumatic events, when going through such a trauma, you need your friends by your side. So, is ignoring what is happening to them the right way to react? Is it helpful to anyone?

We are all individuals, and we deal with things differently. But I hope that when you have finished reading this book, I will at least have given you an insight into what it can sometimes feel like for a cancer patient. If you are someone who would generally disappear, hopefully, I have made you realise how harmful it can be for your friend or family and your future friendship, and you won't disappear. Is it worth losing that person in your life and making them feel you have deserted them? Making them face this alone?

Throughout this journal, I have tried to explain my thoughts and feelings. Due to the severity of some of the side effects, my brain went into self-preservation mode and has shut out a lot of what happened. Therefore, some of what is written is through speaking to others close to me while I went through this ordeal.

Whatever you choose to do, whether you decide you cannot cope and run for the hills or stay put and support your friend/s, I hope you will find the words in this book helpful.

I also thought it would be helpful to have some input from some of the people who helped me get through, so throughout this book, you will find some anecdotes and thoughts from my friends.

Not only is it important for the person who has been diagnosed with his awful disease to be supported, but it is also important for those supporting them to find a way to support themselves at the same time.

At the back of the book, under 'Medical Explanations,' you will find just that: explanations in technical terms via an online search of some of the procedures and side effects associated with medications and treatment. I have marked each one with '*' to make it easier to identify if you want to read about them in more detail. These explanations will give you a better understanding of what is involved.

I also want to add, as it is essential to point out, that my side effects and ongoing problems are at the extreme end of the scale, and not everyone will be as ill as I have been. So, this is probably as bad as it gets. Hopefully, your journey will be much smoother than I experienced!

LIFE CHANGING EVENTS

For most people, I believe that when you look back through the events of your life, there is one traumatic or euphoric incident that is used as a baseline for your personal history. For instance, before we married..., after (child) was born..., etc. Without realising it, we use these 'baselines' to break our lives into more manageable chapters, much like reading a book. I assume that my 'chapters' were once, like almost everyone else's: marriage, the birth of a first child, divorce, second marriage, and the birth of a second child.

But in early 2011, all of that changed; my incredible Mum was diagnosed with breast cancer, and the bottom dropped out of my world.

I lived in Wiltshire, whilst my husband's family and mine lived in North Devon, a distance of roughly 120 miles or three hours, depending on which road you travelled. My immediate knee-jerk reaction was, "... I wanted to be with my family, and we are moving home to Devon..." We never did follow through with this. Although, we seriously considered it and viewed a few houses in Barnstaple. But when we worked out the logistics involved in moving. Besides the physical move and adding an extra 2-3 hours to Simon's travel time, we also needed to consider the stress of uprooting the kids. Then I would also need to find a new job as I didn't think my curtain-making business would be as busy or profitable there. So, we never did move back to Devon, and it proves that acting on an impulse isn't always the best thing to do.

My poor Mum had to have surgery to remove the tumour; this operation is medically termed a lumpectomy*. She ended up needing two operations, as they hadn't excised enough good tissue around the site of the tumour, meaning that, in all likelihood, some cancerous cells could have remained and then continued to grow. She also had two lymph nodes removed, which luckily came back as being non-cancerous so that no further operations would be required. Next came the six treatments of chemotherapy, spaced three weeks apart. Her hair fell out, and she felt awful for the ten days immediately following her treatment. However, once they were out of the way, and although she still wasn't feeling 100%, she found the strength and the energy to continue her passion for horse riding. I would phone her daily when she was over the worst of the side effects and would visit as often as I could, usually staying with my younger sister Faye.

Whilst this was going on, I always said 'before mum's diagnoses' when speaking about past events, so you would assume that this would be my primary 'baseline', but then something even more traumatic happened that affected the entire family and something that we still haven't fully recovered from. Just before Mum was due to start her radiotherapy treatment, Faye was killed in a traffic accident. I won't go into the details as I cannot speak about it, even to this day.

My Mum, who was present at the time, wasn't severely injured, but she suffered a broken wrist, which required an operation to have a pin put in to keep the bone together whilst it healed. But despite this injury and no doubt being in incredible pain, she did everything she could to help Faye.

I feared that Mum would give up and refuse any further treatment, but thankfully, she didn't, and she is still with us, fighting fit and still riding her beloved horse.

So now my baseline for over a decade has been 'before/after Faye' forget the marriages, the births, the divorce, the loss of grandparents. This event was the one traumatic incident that changed my chapters and reduced them from several to just two. Putting it down on paper seems silly, but that is how it is and how it has been for years.

DIAGNOSIS

I have always enjoyed writing. I love how words can feed the imagination and take you to places you never thought possible. It amazes me how you can live someone's life by simply reading the words they have written within the pages of a book and how easy it can be to find solace and excitement in the sentences carefully formed and placed on the paper.

By writing down my innermost thoughts and feelings, I am trying to understand what I have faced, how far I have come, and how much further I still have to go. While I have a fantastic support network behind me, who will always be there regardless, there are some things you don't want to burden people with. So this is my cathartic exercise, my release, my way of coming to terms with everything I have been through and everything that I still have to face.

Allow me to begin with the unburdening of myself.

Sometime during June or July 2022 (the date eludes me now), I found a small lump in my right breast. I wasn't overly concerned as it was in the same place as one that I had investigated years ago, which, after a mammogram and ultrasound, turned out to be a hormonal cyst. So, initially, I dismissed it. After a few weeks, I realised that it was still there. Although I still believed that it was hormonal because, after all, being 47, menopause is just around the corner for me, I decided it would probably be best to get it checked; better safe than sorry, so they say.

5th September 2022 - My first appointment with the nurse at my Doctor's surgery.
After having two children by Caesarean section (yes, the nurses really do shave you before surgery), any thoughts of retaining some form of dignity with medical professions have long gone. However, I still appreciated that the nurse pulled the paper curtain around me whilst I undressed in an attempt to preserve my dignity.

The nurse entered the curtained area, and whilst I stood in front of her, eye to nipple, so to speak, started with a visual examination first, pointing out that one breast is larger than the other, as is usual with all women, to which I confirmed which is the larger. Then, following her instructions and lying down on the bed, she began manipulating and feeling around the area where I'd felt the lump; she also checked the rest of my breast and, for good measure, checked the other one as well. She confirmed that, yes, she could feel the lump as well and that I am probably correct that it is due to hormones. Still, it is always best to err on the side of caution with these things, and she will refer me for a follow-up appointment at the Royal United Hospital (RUH) in Bath. I should hear from them in a couple of weeks.

6th September 2022 - a telephone call from the Royal United Hospital (RUH).
An appointment had been made for the following week, 12th September. I was surprised at how quickly it had come through. After all, it's just a hormonal cyst, right? However, I was pretty pleased that the appointment was on the 12th as well because, on the 13th, I was travelling to Northumberland with some wonderful friends from the paranormal community for a three-day investigation. Yes, I know, I'm one of 'them' - a paranormal nut job!

I continued my everyday life, enjoying my job as a seamstress, not overly concerned with how fast this was moving.

7th September 2022 - Tash
Tash is one of my oldest friends. I have known her since moving to Wiltshire in 2001, and she has been one of my closest companions throughout this time. She has been there through the 'teenage years' with both of my children, my Mum's cancer battle, and the loss of my sister, and she has supported me through it all. I, in turn, have supported her through some of the most challenging times in her life, including the loss of her own Mum to cancer.

Because we are so close, almost like sisters, and tell each other everything, she knew something was wrong the minute she entered my front door. It is Wednesday, our weekly 'treat night'. This started years ago when we began attending Fat Club; everyone else would probably refer to it as a slimming club, but we preferred the ring of Fat Club, so it stayed. After standing on the scales, we would treat ourselves, regardless of whether we had lost or put on, irrespective of the fact that we probably had already had a treat that week. Before Covid, we decided to ditch going to a fat club and do it at my house instead; we'd stand on the scales and stuff our faces with lots of delectable treats, usually consisting of two desserts! Post-COVID, we continued with treat night but ditched the scales, which probably explains our continuously expanding waistlines!

I told her I had found a lump, which was being investigated, but not to worry because it was probably just a cyst. One of the many reasons I love Tash is that she, like myself, has no filter and says precisely what she's thinking. 'Let us have a feel then' is her first response, then, 'can't feel anything, must be in your head, anyway let's change the subject because it isn't all about you, you know'. Her bluntness makes me laugh and takes my mind away from it. It would have made it ten times worse for me if she had been emotional. After being sworn to secrecy, as I didn't want anyone worrying about me on my account, she started to moan about dinner not being ready, as I 'only had one job'. This is a weekly occurrence in my house; the fact that I haven't made or planned anything for dinner is a longstanding joke, as is my timekeeping.

8th September 2022 - Karin

I was on my way home from Fat Club; after realising that I should really at least try to get my waistline under control, I had rejoined a few weeks previous to this and would go on 5 - 8 mile walks each evening in an attempt to shift the pounds, when Karin had called. Sensing that I am distracted, I tell her that I have found a lump, and in usual Karin fashion, she takes my mind away from it by making me laugh as she begins to insult me. Some of you will find this strange, but I find insults funny; the ruder and further below the 'line of decency', the better.

I met Karin over a decade ago at an investigation in Glastonbury. I'm rubbish with names and called her Kristina all night, but she never once corrected me. Knowing her as well as I do now, she probably found it hilarious while thinking I was a blithering idiot.

We have the same sense of humour and love insulting each other. We laugh constantly when in each other's company and recite lines from our favourite comedians and films. Our other friends would sometimes look at us in fits of laughter, wondering what the hell happened and why are there two of them.

She has the ability to make you laugh until your stomach hurts.

Along with my daily walks, I signed for and was in training for the Bath Half Marathon. I was making small changes in my life to get fitter and slimmer. Looking back, I suppose that this was an attempt to fit in with the mainstream rhetoric for what is considered acceptable to be happy.

9th September 2022 - Sally
I have known Sally for over a decade. She is one of my 'sewing friends. 'I have very few friends who sew, so having someone like Sally in my life has been amazing. I met her when I worked in a local fabric and haberdashery shop. She ran quilting workshops while I served customers behind the counter.

Through our love of sewing, we have become firm friends. Despite being over 20 years my senior, she is young at heart, so mentally, we are the same age. I've always seen her as an extraordinary friend; she gives excellent advice and makes the most amazing cakes and soups.

Telling Sally my health worries was hard, but she kept me occupied and focused on the task at hand throughout the day.

12th September 2022 - First appointment at the Royal United Hospital (RUH)
Simon came with me to the RUH. The hospital is very well laid out and has a cafe located right outside the Breast Unit, so I deposited him there with a cup of coffee. No sooner had I turned my back than he had cracked open his laptop and started work. The only upside to Simon working remotely is that he could attend all my appointments without them interfering with his career. I went in for my appointment alone because it's just a cyst, right?

Again, the same procedure as I had at the Doctor's: visual inspection, manipulation and kneading, but this time, I had to place my hand on her shoulder whilst she felt around my armpit.

She agreed with me that there was indeed something there, and yes, although it is probably hormonal, it is best to get it checked out. So, the nurse referred me for a mammogram and ultrasound, and she told me that I should hear from the hospital with an appointment in three to five weeks. I left the breast unit, collected Simon, and we made our way home. Neither of us was seemingly concerned, believing it was a cyst and that they were following protocol.

During the drive home, apart from our initial conversation when leaving the hospital, we didn't speak. Both of us were wrapped up in our thoughts of the tasks that we still had to do that day. Simon's thoughts were undoubtedly the number of conference calls he needed to sit in on, while mine were focused on mentally packing my case for tomorrow.

13th September 2022 - Crystal
I have known Crystal for almost 20 years; she is one of the kindest people I know, and she would drop everything to be there for you. We are off to Chillingham Castle in Northumberland today, and she arrives at my house early so we can have a coffee and a quick catch-up whilst waiting for Selina to arrive. The three of us are travelling together, with me playing chauffeur extraordinaire. She senses that something is off, and I

tell her that I've found a lump and am beginning to worry but not to tell anyone. She gives me the tightest hug possible, and I can't help but cry a little. Crystal had lost her wonderful Dad to cancer earlier this year, so emotions are still very raw for anyone who knew him. I, for one, will miss his usual greeting of 'god it's her, time we were heading home' whenever I visited. As I said before, I am not normal.

13th - 16th December 2022 - Chillingham Castle

This little paranormal break has been planned for over a year, and it couldn't have come at a better time. Admittedly, when I clicked 'going', I didn't know where it was. My sense of geography is ridiculous, and I often joke that I could get lost in a brown paper bag, even with directions. Someone told me that it is near Scotland, so as far as I was concerned, I was going to Scotland, and I took great delight in telling people that I was driving all the way to Scotland.

We spent the days investigating the local area, visiting Holy Island and Bamburgh Castle, where we signed the condolence book for Queen Elizabeth II. The nights were spent investigating Chillingham Castle. We didn't find any conclusive evidence that ghosts are real--we never do--but we all had a fantastic time away with great friends.

Sometime during these few days away, my Dad, who had recently been undergoing cancer treatment, phoned with the news that he had been given the all-clear. I cried tears of relief as I hung up the phone; Crystal looked at me and, fearing the worst, said, 'All okay?' I told her that my Dad had been given the all-clear, and she hugged me and began to cry; all I could say to her was, 'I'm sorry'. So picture, if you will: two grown women standing in the courtyard of Chillingham Castle, bawling their eyes out, one saying 'I'm so pleased for you', whilst the other is saying she's 'sorry'.

28th September 2022 - phone call from the Royal United Hospital

I was on my way to a client to measure for curtains and blinds when I received a call from the Breast Unit at the hospital. "We have a last-minute appointment tomorrow morning. Would you be able to come?"

I managed to find a safe place to pull the car over to continue the call and check my already full diary. I decided to cancel all my morning appointments. I told them, "Yes, of course, I'll be there."

The nurse on the other end of the phone advised me not to wear perfume or deodorant, as they could interfere with the readings. The one thought in my head was,' Christ, I'm going to stink!' which really should have been the least of my worries.

I do not know how, but I managed to forget about the looming appointment and continue to my client's home. I only got lost once, so that is a win as far as I am concerned.

29th September 2022 - Second appointment at the RUH

When I arrived at the hospital and after I had deposited my husband in the cafe with his laptop so that he could continue to work, I walked through the door of the Breast Unit and checked in at reception. Sitting in the waiting area, I began playing games on my phone.

My name was called, and as I looked up, I saw a lady standing there, notes in hand, waiting for me. She introduced herself as I approached, and I know it's awfully rude of me, but I cannot remember her name. She told me that she would perform my mammogram today.

If you haven't had a mammogram* before, it's a little difficult to adequately explain the sensations that you will experience whilst undergoing one. Yes, we all joke that your boob gets flattened, which, essentially, is correct. What they fail to mention to you is that your boob is carefully manhandled and pulled and tugged into position. A clear piece of Perspex, which is part of the machine, is inched ever closer to your breast until it is in the perfect position. The piece of Perspex is then clamped down onto your breast with all the pressure of a vice. You are then advised not to move or breathe while taking the image. Trust me, if you were to try to move, you would probably leave half, if not all, of your breast behind! It isn't an enjoyable experience but a means to an end.

After the mammogram image was taken, I returned to the waiting area until my name was called for my ultrasound. I pulled out my phone and continued my Nonogram puzzle game; deep in thought of whether to place a box or a cross, I heard my name called again. Looking up, I was quite surprised to see the same lady who had performed my mammogram. She took me to one side and told me that they wanted to take some more detailed images of my right breast. My initial thought was, 'This doesn't bode well', but I still believed that it was hormonal and that they were just being thorough. In hindsight, after the second set of images was taken, I should have retrieved my husband from the cafe, but I didn't.

Again, I am ushered back to the waiting room, and again, I am deep in thought, playing my game, when my name is called for a third time. I follow the nurse--again, her name evades me--to the ultrasound room. The ultrasound is similar to one that you would have during pregnancy; it is just on a different part of your anatomy.

During my ultrasound, the lovely lady performing the ultra-sound said, 'I won't lie to you. You're right. There is something there; we women know our breasts. I am going to take three samples for a biopsy*.' It took a while for my brain to catch up, 'so this isn't a cyst?' I remember her telling me that I would have a local anaesthetic at the biopsy sight; they would take three samples from my breast and one from an enlarged lymph node. With tears running down my face, they performed the biopsy procedure, removing the samples that they needed.

The nurses were all amazing, and they spoke to me the whole time to distract me. Not about the procedure, but what I did for a living, how far I had come to get to the hospital, and how full the carpark was--just mundane everyday things. But to be honest with you, in that situation, I could have had front-row seats to a private viewing of the Chippendales or the Dream Boys wiggling at me; nothing could have distracted me from the thoughts whirling around in my head, 'I have cancer', 'I am going to die', 'what about my kids?', 'what about Simon?' and underneath all of this a little voice screaming 'FUUUCCCKKKKKK!' I am sure that I am not alone in having these thoughts when you first hear that you have a cancer diagnosis.

After the Doctor had put a significant amount of pressure on the biopsy site to stem the flow of blood and I had been patched up, I dutifully got dressed in a daze. I was asked if I had attended my appointment on my own; luckily, I hadn't, and I couldn't wait to see Simon so that he could reassure me that I would be fine and, together, we would get through this. My ultrasound doctor said that she would check when my surgeon was free and asked if I would be willing to wait around to see her. Apparently, it makes the whole process easier for the next stage. Of course, I elected to wait, needing as much information as possible. However, when I met my surgeon, I couldn't think of a single thing to say.

Walking in a shocked daze through the Breast Unit towards the cafe, the only thought on my mind was to be strong and try not to break down in public. Looking over the sea of heads, I found Simon sitting in front of his laptop, headphones on, listening to whatever drivel his employer was requesting, with a half-drunk cup of coffee and an empty sandwich wrapper beside him. Looking up as I approached him, the words' ready to go?' died on his lips; one look at my face told him all he needed to know.

'We have to go back in to see the surgeon.'

Straight away, he is on autopilot. 'Right, okay, all good?' His face briefly shows shock and panic.

The word 'no' catches in my throat, and I shake my head.

Quickly packing away his laptop and disposing of his coffee and sandwich wrapper in the bin, we walked hand in hand back through the doors of the Breast Unit. Standing in the now-empty waiting area, we held each other, waiting for my name to be called to see the surgeon. The same thoughts circled in my head, and I'm almost positive that Simon was thinking the same.

The image association of such a simple six-letter word is horrendous and affects everyone: the patient, their family, and their friends.

The phrase' silence is deafening' seems so ridiculous a statement, until, of course, you have experienced it for yourself, and for me, the silence in the empty waiting room was deafening. It was as if time had frozen, and the only two people left in existence were myself and Simon, my husband and best friend. We were desperately clinging to each other, wanting to rewind the clock instead of having to wait to discuss the options that were soon to be laid out in front of us.

We were called in to see our surgeon; I say we, because, after all, 'we' will have to face this together and support each other through it as best we can. Taking a seat at the end of her desk, I try not to make eye contact with her because, stupidly, that would make it seem real, and I am not ready to face the reality of this. Growing up, I was likened to Peter Pan, as I never wanted to grow up, whether that is because I didn't want to face the adult world or whether it was because I felt unprepared for the reality of how cruel people can be to one another, I do not know. I tell you this to help you understand that I have spent most of my adult life with blinkers on, refusing to admit the reality of adult life, and now the blinkers were being forcibly and painfully removed.

Our surgeon seemed lovely, and speaking slowly, she explained the next steps. From the scans, my tumour is 30mm x 26mm x

16mm; in my head, I think that it is about the size of a broad bean. Now, I wouldn't say I like broad beans, and certainly, I wouldn't say I like this parasite growing inside of me. The technical term for it is DCIS, or Ductal Carcinoma InSitu, which means that it is in one place, the milk duct and hasn't spread to another area of the breast, which apparently is good news. The not-so-good news is that it appears to have spread to my lymph nodes. I am by no means stupid, and I know that this news is not good. My husband is sitting beside me, frantically taking as many notes as possible, whilst I am sitting there trying to focus on remaining positive instead of latching on to the dark thoughts of 'I am going to die' 'I am going to leave Simon a widower' "my children will be orphans' etc., I'm sure that you can get the gist, I started practising my new mantra, 'it's going to be fine' 'you're going to be fine' 'it's all going to be okay' 'they are probably wrong anyway, it is just a cyst' even now, I still think that it's a cyst. It's either positive thinking, denial, or Peter Pan syndrome; who knows?

My immediate, knee-jerk reaction is to have a mastectomy. But unable to formulate the words, I ask the surgeon just to cut my tit off; I have two beautiful children, so it is now surplus to requirements. With a kind smile and gentle words, she explained to me that if that is what I truly want to happen, then they will do it, but she asked me to give it some careful consideration because living without a breast is not an easy thing to do. She proceeded to tell me that as my lymph nodes have been affected, I will need chemotherapy regardless of what surgery I have. Remembering what my poor Mum went through over a decade ago and how ill she was whilst undergoing treatment filled me with dread. But if she could do it, then so can I!

To be honest, most of what the surgeon said fell on deaf ears; I remember Simon asking if it was curable, which, silly as it sounds, wasn't something I had even considered asking. As much as they can tell you, for fear of being sued, she reassured us that most breast cancers are survivable.

As we left, she asked about our children and whether we would tell them yet. We have always believed in telling our children the truth, no matter how painful it may be. Because if you don't, they will find the answers to their questions, and if they discover that you have previously lied to them, they may no longer trust you. We told her we would tell them as soon as we saw them; she responded that it was a good thing, as kids always know when something is wrong.

We travelled the 30-40 minutes home in almost complete silence, both of us trying to make sense of how on earth our world could be ripped apart so quickly. Luckily, Simon was driving, as I do not think I would have been mentally capable at that moment in time; he occasionally squeezed my knee to offer support. We agree that we will tell Harrison, our 17-year-old son when he gets home from school; when I say we, I obviously mean Simon. Our adult daughter, Rachael, is currently on holiday with her partner Jamie. They had recently discovered that they are pregnant, so this will be the last holiday they will be going on for a while. Not wanting to ruin it for them, rightly or wrongly, we decide to tell them when they get back and collect the girls, their two pugs, to whom I am affectionately referred as nanny. They plan on both coming to collect them, so at least Rach won't have to travel nearly an hour home alone.

We already suspected how they would both react; Harrison, being autistic, would be as cool as a cucumber, whereas Rach would break down.

Arriving home, we have some time before Harrison returns from school. He is doing his A-levels, and I am so proud of how, considering everything he's been through, he is getting excellent grades. I start by video calling my parents, first my Mum, who doesn't pick up; not wanting to delay telling people and getting it out in the open, I call my Dad and step Mum, Sue. They both looked like the bottom had dropped out of their world, and my Dad immediately offered to come up. Being pragmatic, I tell him, 'No, that there is nothing he can do, and I would worry about him driving all this way'. But whilst I was speaking with him, there was a little girl inside me, screaming that she wanted a hug from her daddy. My Mum burst into tears, uttering the word 'no' repeatedly. Telling your parents, who have both had cancer, that you have just been diagnosed is one of the hardest things that I have had to do so far in my life. My sister Jo, who I had been unable to get hold of, and after no doubt receiving calls from both of our parents, called me. She offered to come up and asked how the kids had taken it, to which I said I'd let her know.

I'm not the sort of person who likes to cause problems or trouble in people's lives, so telling people this news was really hard for me. I don't want to think of people worrying about me, either, so although a few close friends knew that I was having some tests done, I didn't broadcast it. I had to tell the kids first, then decide whether I would go public.

Harrison came home from school to find both his parents sat in stunned silence, waiting for his return. Simon was incredibly strong and laid out the facts that we knew to Harrison; he took it like an absolute trooper. I assured him that I was going to be absolutely fine. He grabbed a mountain of food and disappeared to his room, no doubt to start researching my diagnosis. If Harrison had reacted differently to our news than I had expected, it would have made things ten times worse for me.

4th October 2022 - Telling Rach and Jamie

We have spent the last few days going through the motions and waiting for Rach to return. We discreetly tried to determine if Jamie was still coming with her when she picked up the girls. Unfortunately, their plans had changed, so we had no option but to track them on 'find my friends' and then video call them when we saw they were home. Rach took the news precisely as expected and then began cleaning her already clean kitchen as denial set in. Her partner, Jamie, was and is amazing. Despite being stunned, he tried to continue a normal conversation while we asked them for the details of their holiday.

Understandably, Rachael was cross with us for not telling her as soon as we found out. But, rightly or wrongly, we didn't want to ruin their holiday. I have been where Rach is now, and when I found out, I wanted to drop everything and be with my Mum to support her. I didn't want Rach to spend the last few days of her holiday worrying about me or, even worse, cutting her holiday short, so I stand by our decision to wait until they returned.

5th October 2022 - Telling my remaining friends
Now that Rach and Jamie know, I can begin telling everyone else.

Tash was utterly stunned and couldn't stay on the phone for long, so she needed time to compose herself. She called me back once she could, and I told her the options. She said, 'Just cut it off; it's not like you need it anymore' I reiterated what the surgeon had said about it not being easy living with one breast and that there isn't a guarantee that breast reconstruction can work, plus I would need to wait at least two years after treatment.

Karin went into personal assistant mode and started asking lots of questions whilst poking fun and making me laugh. Her cousin Marianne had had cancer during lockdown, and with my permission, Karin sent my number to her, just in case I wanted to speak to someone else who had gone through it. Karin is brilliant at bringing people together. She is very much 'Do you have a problem? Here this person will fix' (said in a 'Don't mess with the Zohan' accent, which is one of our favourite films. We quote some of the lines and break into fits of laughter whilst our friends are wondering what the hell just happened) I asked her to inform some of our paranormal friends, as I didn't want them finding out through the grapevine. Or to have continual messages asking about my absence. I also knew that these people would support Karin and each other. Despite her hard exterior, she has a very soft centre, a bit like an armadillo.
After telling Crystal of my cancer diagnosis, she wanted to come straight around, but at this point, I was so exhausted from worry and lack of sleep that I wasn't really in the right frame of mind for visitors. Something I actually regret is not allowing her to visit

me; hindsight is a wonderful thing, as at this stage, I didn't realise that it would be some time before I would see her again.

I phoned Sally and told her my news; she was as shocked as I was because she believed it to be hormonal, like me. I told her that I had to go back the following week and tell them which course of treatment I wanted to have.

I visited two other couples I have known for years and have become firm friends with. One couple was shocked and thought I had come to tell them that Rach was pregnant. She is, but it is not my place to go public with it until she is ready to. Whilst one member of the other couple had a complete meltdown, I had to tell them to go away and compose themselves as it didn't help either of us. I may have come across as a bit of a bitch, but I didn't want anyone crying or worrying about me.

Because in my head the tumour is about the size of a broad bean, and because I detest broad beans, I set up a messenger group with my paranormal friends called 'Bean Faced B*****d', with strict instructions that I do not want their sympathy; I want insults with lashings of rudeness. Most of them have read my self-published erotic fiction, so they know that there is no limit to how rude they can be.

In addition to being a paranormal investigator, I am also a member of the Jamaica Inn Paranormal Team, and I have been since 2019. I absolutely love this place. All the staff are so friendly and work incredibly hard to ensure that all their guests have a fantastic time. If you are ever in Cornwall, I recommend visiting for a meal or looking around the Smugglers Museum, gift shop, or farm shop.

7th October 2022 - Biopsy results
I can honestly say that I have barely slept or have been able to eat for the past eight days. I would go to bed and, with the aid of a prescription to help me sleep, would drift off but wake again in the small hours. Unable to stem the tears that would flow freely, afraid that the sound would wake Simon, I would creep

downstairs and sob quietly until there was nothing left in me. My ribs would hurt from the dry heaving my racking sobs produced, and would finally fall asleep from exhaustion on the sofa. I would wake each morning with a blanket carefully placed over me by my forever-caring husband.

D-day has arrived, the biopsy results are in, and it is time to decide on which treatment route I'll be taking. During the meeting with our surgeon, she told us what type of cancer I have. It is an aggressive, fast-growing variety, and it is definitely in at least one of my lymph nodes. There are three choices of treatment; option one is a mastectomy, chemotherapy* and then radiotherapy*, option two is a mammoplasty* (similar to a breast reduction, but they remove the tumour and rejig all of the breast tissue, the breast is made smaller and the nipple is relocated), chemotherapy, then radiotherapy, or option three; chemotherapy in a bid to reduce the size of the tumour, surgery (a choice of two, depending on how effective the chemotherapy is at reducing the size of the tumour) and then radiotherapy.

It astounded me and still does that they make the patient decide which road to take. After all, they are the experts and have all the information in front of them, so they should know from experience the best course of action for each patient. But I suppose they are so afraid of being sued and having a black mark against their name that they negate responsibility by making the patient choose.

All I could focus on was 'fast-growing', 'aggressive', and 'lymph nodes'. To be honest, when deciding which route you choose to go down, you will never know if it is the right option until you get to the end. But with these three words stuck on repeat in my head, I chose option three. At least then, if it has spread elsewhere, fingers crossed, the chemotherapy will kill it.

The breast care nurse took both myself and my husband to another room. She gently explained to us that it would be 8 - 9 months of treatment and that most people don't work through it. I was shocked and didn't think I could survive without working. I love my job; playing with fabric and making beautiful window treatments for my lovely clients puts me in a happy place. Even through Covid, when work dried up, I found a way of being in my happy place by making scrubs and scrub bags for the NHS.

She armed us with lots of leaflets and booklets, giving us all the information we could possibly require, and with all of our questions answered, we left the hospital. I called my kids, parents, sister, and close friends. By the time I arrived home, I was done talking about it; I messaged a few friends who would message me frequently, asking how I was without expecting an immediate answer. You know the ones, we all have them, the ones that make you feel relevant in their lives.

From here on out, there would be a steady stream of mail from the hospital. My next appointment is booked for 12th October and will be to meet my Oncologist, who will explain the first stage of my chemotherapy treatment.

12th October 2022 - Oncology appointment and discussion of treatment

Attending my appointment with the Oncologist, I was surprised to be asked to wear a mask, considering that COVID is considered as nothing worse than the flu now. I am also soon to discover that oncologists are always running late, I suppose with even the best will in the world, if you are having to give a patient bad news you can hardly kick them out of your office because their appointment time is up.

After nearly an hour of waiting in a hospital waiting room, on a chair as comfortable as you can find in a hospital waiting room, a nurse called us to a secondary waiting area. After waiting for what felt like a lifetime, we were beginning to get a bit concerned that we had been forgotten about. Alas, it may just have been wishful thinking, as my name is called, and we are led into a fair-sized office.

The consultant reels off a list of possible side effects, nausea, fatigue, weight loss/ gain, compromised immunity, ulcers, thrush (both ends), and then looking me in the eye, she tells me that with this treatment, I will lose my hair, which is what hit me the hardest. Even though, to the disgust of my hairdresser, I rarely look after it properly, generally, after washing it, I'd put it straight up into a ponytail whilst still wet, yanking at it with my hairbrush to get the abundance of knots out that I would always seem to get. Out of all the other possible side effects, the fact that I would loose my hair broke my heart.

The Oncologist gives me a consent form to read and sign while the consultant finds a nurse to take my blood. I didn't even read it; I just signed. After reading it entirely, I don't think anyone will refuse treatment; sometimes ignorance is bliss, or so they say. Simon, however, did read it. I just looked at him and told him that I didn't want to know.

Everything is moving so quickly, and I am booked in to start my treatment on Monday in just five day's time. Whilst I am pleased that it is moving forward so quickly, in the back of my head, I can't help but think that they aren't telling me something.

Bloods are taken from my crappy veins; they have always been problematic in allowing blood to be taken. They like to fool the phlebotomist that they have struck gold, only to say 'nah, nah, nah, nah, nah' as the vial comes up empty. This nurse is the first one I have met who has been able to get blood out of me on the first go; my veins clearly like her. She takes me on a tour of the area where I will receive my treatment, and I meet some of the staff; they all seem lovely and are very cheery and friendly.

On the way home, there are phone calls to be made, one to our son, to let him know that we'll be home soon. It's a Wednesday, which means that Tash is already at our home and has now started cooking dinner for the four of us. Then there are the phone calls to Rachael, my Mum, my Dad, my sister, Tash, and Karin. These people are my family and little did I realise it then, but after each treatment, as soon as we were in the car and heading home from the hospital, I would make the round-robin of phone calls and texts, telling them all that I'm okay and that we are on our way home.

To be honest, up to this point, I suppose I must have been in shock. The world had been turning, but I wasn't present. Yes, I spoke to people, and I continued to work, trying to complete as many orders as possible, but I wasn't present. I was just going through the motions. Someone could suggested that I sell both of my kidneys on the black market and I would have agreed, and I would have had no clue.

The following five days drag endlessly ahead of us; we try to keep busy, although for the life of me, I cannot recall what we did. I remember that my phone became my new best friend as I played endless rounds of Nonogram until my weary eyes refused to focus any longer. During these five days, I received another letter from the hospital asking for an appointment with the Oncologist again. My heart made a swift move vertically, and with it firmly planted in my mouth, I read the letter over and over again, the whole time thinking that they'd found something else and that the cancer had spread elsewhere in my body, so my number has been called, and my ticket has been stamped, get ready for departure.

16th October 2022 - Narva

We all have friends that we drift apart from. They don't stop being your friends, but life takes over, and you don't see or contact them as much as you should. Narva is one of these friends. She is also another kind soul whom I am forever thankful to have in my life. Although I hadn't seen her for what felt like a lifetime, she was actually in Rome when I broke the news to her. But I didn't want her to find out through word of mouth or online.

Suspecting how I must be feeling, she visited me out of the blue on her return, with a gift she called a 'chemo care package' inside I found my favourite chocolates and jelly sweets, and a card telling me how strong I am and 'you've got this, and we've got you'. Her visits with 'chemo care packages' were a regular occurrence; sometimes, they would contain skin care, new pyjamas, or cakes. But always the same message: 'You've got this, and we've got you'.

She would frequently call me if she was going shopping to ask if there was anything that I wanted, and then she would deliver it to my doorstep. She is also a qualified nurse, although she doesn't practice it anymore, so she knew exactly how ill I was on her frequent visits.

Speaking with her now, I tell her that she has no idea how much these simple acts of kindness and thoughtfulness helped me through. She tells me she doesn't 'think she did enough,' but I honestly think she did too much.

THOUGHTS FROM MY FAMILY

Despite mentioning this journal to my mum and Dad and explaining why I felt compelled to share my story, I didn't ask them outright if they would be willing to write something about the process and how it felt for them, being so close to me and going through everything.

The reason for this is self-preservation for them. For parents who have not only gone through cancer themselves, and knowing what mental mind fuck it can be, but also parents who have lost one daughter and then have to face the possibility of losing another one, I don't feel it would have been fair for me to ask this of them.

My stepmum Sue, has a very methodical brain. After my sister passed, she was brilliant at sorting everything out. Just being able to, in a way, detach yourself from what was going on to get the task done, so I knew she would be willing to write from her perspective what it is like for families looking in.

RACHAEL

There are only a few times in life that you lose your breath completely! This could be from playing a sport like boxing or when your world gets wiped from your feet instantly - this was my scenario.

Coming back from holiday, after finding out mum has Cancer! I remember it like it was yesterday. I think it haunts me sometimes; I was hyperventilating so badly and remember thinking this wasn't good for the baby I was growing inside of me. I felt so scared and angry at the whole situation. Why my mum? We had so many plans, but as time wore on, Mum became so sick, I think she forgets how poorly she truly was. I also think she forgets how far she's come and what a fucking hero she is! (sorry, I have a potty mouth)

My family is as mad as a box of frogs, but I'm incredibly proud to have them.

My Dad - he's normally not very good in situations where you show emotions, same as my partner Jamie, but he has been my mum's rock during this all. He doesn't get enough credit, but I want him to know I'm proud of him. Although there was time, we thought we'd need to plan Mum's funeral and what would happen if she didn't make it. but she's here. So here's to living the best life possible with the best family. (Please don't shave your hair again dad, Shit hair and a shit dress sense don't go) Love you Dad!!

Harry - my baby brother, although you tower over me and outsmart me on a weekly basis, I know you struggled with it all, but we tried to protect you as much as we knew how. Your humour, wit and positivity were unmatched. I can't wait to see where life takes you as you get older after such a shit time! This has brought us closer as we always checked in daily with each other. Just know we love you and have your back, you lanky bastard!

Jay - my partner, who again handled everything so bloody well. You helped dress Mum, wheel Mum around the hospital, make sure Harrison was okay, and stay grounded and as calm as you could during my pregnancy. Thank you for being my rock! I couldn't have stayed so strong without you. PS You're the best, Dad!

Friends - thank you for letting me cry all the time, for the check-ins, and for the positivity you gave me. I'm forever grateful.

Frankie - you are my saving grace. You will never know how much you kept me and Nanny going. I feel so lucky to have you, and I am so lucky that Nanny got to meet you and watch you grow! We all love you lots.

My mum - my best friend 2.0 has arrived, and I'm so proud of you. Not once did you moan about how much pain you were in or how scared you were. You laughed throughout, and I admire you so much. I'm so lucky you're here to see Frankie grow, as I honestly didn't think you would be!

Here's to you and making all the memories we can! I love you. Here's to a second chance!

If anyone is struggling with the effects of cancer, please talk to someone. You're not weak for crying or wanting help; it affects everyone! I know it's easier said than done, but try and treat the person who has cancer as normal as possible. Try to laugh when you can, but also try and look after yourself as well.

Rach xxx

HARRISON

When I got home from school, Mum and Dad were sitting in the lounge in silence. This was strange, as normally they would have been upstairs working. The room felt still, and I knew that something was wrong.

Dad told me that Mum had breast cancer, and I was completely shocked. I didn't know that she was undergoing investigation for this, and I didn't realise that there was anything wrong with her until this point. They reassured me that everything was going to be ok.

I went to my room and sat quietly; I would normally have listened to some music or spoken with friends.

Dad offered to tell the school what was happening, but initially, I didn't want him to. As Mum's condition worsened and my studies slipped, I decided to let Dad tell them. At least they would understand why sometimes I could not concentrate in lessons.

As Mum's immune system was gone, I was worried about making her ill; I would speak to her from a distance.

Eventually, it became impossible for me to attend school, as COVID was still in circulation along with other illnesses that spread like wildfire in the School environment. The School were very understanding and agreed that I could resit my current year. I would still be one of their pupils, but it was our choice whether I attended lessons.

Watching Mum go through treatment, she was very poorly. I would come home from school, and she would be asleep in the lounge.

Mum was admitted to the hospital countless times, and I didn't really understand what was going on. I would be woken in the middle of the night by Dad telling me that he was taking Mum to the hospital. It would be radio silence for a few hours and I would find out the following morning if Mum was ok or not. My parents didn't tell me until after each hospital visit what it was for, whether it was a blood test, treatment or an infection.

I remember that Dad once took a sip out of Mum's cup shortly after one of her chemo sessions, and he became ill, suffering from similar symptoms to Mum. So I wouldn't advise doing this. He also lost his eyebrows when Mum was going through chemotherapy, so the toxins must have been coming out of her skin and infecting Dad. Without his eyebrows, he looked like a supervillain from an Austin Powers movie.

When Dad got ill with COVID, I had to take care of both of them. Dad particularly liked my Hot Chocolates, and I would make them for Mum and Dad, although Mum didn't really drink much of hers. To make sure that I checked on them regularly, I set an alarm on my phone. Dad was really poorly, and Mum was admitted to the Hospital. Even when she came home, I would check on her throughout the day. They both stayed in their rooms for over a week; Dad had taken up residence in the spare room when he started feeling unwell, not realising that Mum had already caught it.

I would shake them awake to check that they were still alive; if they didn't wake up immediately, what was probably just a millisecond felt like a lifetime. I always thought that my parents were dead.

Having to do this made me realise how hard it was for Dad to care for Mum twenty-four hours a day. He also had a stressful corporate job and had to keep the house running.

I was used to Mum having to stay at the hospital a lot, but Christmas Day was different. Rachael and Jamie were staying over for the night. I was woken up at roughly 11 pm by Dad telling me that Mum was poorly and that they were taking her to the hospital; Jamie and Rachael were standing in the doorway and told me that Rach was driving Mum and Dad and that J would stay with me. I could tell by Rachs' face that they were all really worried. But I didn't really understand what was happening because it wasn't discussed until much later.

Whenever Mum was in the hospital, Dad and I had a ritual. This developed after I had come downstairs to raid the fridge, and I saw Dad sitting in silence in the lounge, drinking Whisky. He looked destroyed, so I sat with him to keep him company. From this point on, every time Mum was in hospital overnight, Dad and I would sit in silence, keeping each other company while drinking whisky.

I remember that she once asked me to open a bottle for her, as she was so weak and couldn't. As I could not unscrew the bottle, I used my teeth. It worked, but Mum had a complete breakdown, thinking that I was trying to eat the bottle. This is how severely the medication has affected her brain power.

Mum has now finished her treatment, and since stopping the anti-cancer pill, she is more like her old self. Although her mobility has been affected, unfortunately, her sarcasm and mick-taking haven't.

Rachael used to say that Mum is a new mum, Mum 2.0, when she was taking all of the medication. But now it feels like I have my mum back.

SUE

It rocks your world when you hear that someone you love has cancer.

What can you say - it literally renders you speechless. And then you think of something to say and it sounds like some awful crappy cliche.

Lisa told us that she had cancer over a video call - she was crying - we were crying. And I know her Dad was terrified because we all associate the Big C word with death - however much we try not to.

But Lisa's public face of bravery and dignity - literally from Day 1 - made it easier for us to bear even though we knew she must have had dark moments far more often than we ever saw evidence of. So while having cancer and chemo and surgery and radiotherapy and endless hideous and toxic drugs plus her own fear and pain, I truly believe she took a lot of our fear and pain away by being so selfless and unbelievably positive.

I am in awe of her to be honest.

I am not Lisa's "real" mum - but I love her like a real daughter and I am just so happy, relieved and all the other inadequate words that she told cancer to Fuck Off -- and it did!

Sue (Wicked Stepmother) xxx

JOANNE

The minute I received the call from Lisa I was immediately determined that she was going to be ok.

I recall my first words were 'don't worry, don't worry, it will be ok, you know it will' but now feel this was a shocked reaction to the news. Lisa was crying and I had to say anything to stop her and make her feel better (I come from a long line of 'fixers'). Initially I fell into denial, I hoped she had gotten confused and maybe they were wrong but after listening to her for a few minutes the truth sank in.

Throughout this, in fact, throughout all of Lisa's treatment, I have always maintained my refusal to believe she was going to be anything other than alright. I feel this came from the belief that life wouldn't be unkind enough to take two sisters from me! Even now, with the disabilities that she has to endure, I am still utterly convinced that, eventually, she is going to be alright.

My parents were planning to visit Lisa the following day. We were all going to go, but my employer at the time refused to allow me the time off. We were in the midst of budget meetings, and I had to be there to 'work the spreadsheet'. I sat sobbing through those budget meetings, trying to process the news and angry that I had not been permitted to be there to support my sister. I always wonder if the branch managers had been briefed that day because no one drew attention to the ginger sobbing in the corner.

My sister has a dark sense of humour which is the same as my own. I set up a Whatsapp group that our family could share memes and messages to cheer her up during her treatment. With quick succession all of our parents dropped off the group to 'leave us to it'. I would like to say that tempered our posts but I can genuinely state that the meme's got worse from then on in.

I called Lisa almost every day through her treatment, telling her all about the dramas that were surrounding my life at the time. Often, she would need to jump off quickly, either because she couldn't take any more or because she was feeling poorly – who knows.

I think, during this period, I managed to remain positive due to being so resolute that Lisa was going to be fine and that this was just a blip. Even through the sepsis and the hospital stays, that belief did not change. I knew Lisa would fight this and that Faye would definitely not want her up there yet!

Fight she did, and I am so proud of her, not only for getting through this but for everything she achieves.

Despite the fact she is a twat, she is my twat!

Love you to the moon and back (and then a little further) badonkadonk
   Joanne (badinkadink) xxxxx

PICTURES BEFORE DIAGNOSIS

Pictures of myself pre-cancer; lots of fun, laughter, and great times spent with family and friends.

FIRST CHEMOTHERAPY TREATMENT

17th October 2022

I didn't sleep at all the night before my first treatment; my mind was in overdrive, mainly the mantra of 'I don't want to die' 'I don't want to die'. I messaged the BFB (Bean Faced B*****d chat page) with two simple words: 'I'm scared'. The response was overwhelming, 'You'd be stupid if you weren't, and You're not stupid' along with memes of 'facepalm' and 'duh'. Not the usual sentiments of 'you'll be fine' ', try not to worry', etc.; these are my people; they get me.

You don't realise how precious your life is until someone tells you something is trying to take it away. We can all be guilty of going through the motions; some of us may make plans for our retirement, but so many of us may never make it. As my mum has told me countless times, 'Today is a gift; tomorrow isn't promised.'

Arriving at the Oncology department, mask firmly in place, I make my way to the Chemotherapy unit and immediately get lost. I find a friendly nurse who takes me to the unit, which I hasten to point out is clearly signposted. The receptionist greets me with 'first time?' I am absolutely petrified; despite the Hospital sending emails detailing the procedure with a carefully scripted video featuring patients who explain the whole process, I cannot stop the whooshing noise in my ears, which is undoubtedly caused by my racing heart. With fear in my voice, I showed her the most recent appointment letter that I had received. She settled my anxiety by telling me that it is a protocol to have a face-to-face meeting after your first chemotherapy to check how you have responded to the treatment and how you are feeling.

I am shown to a small sink and given instructions to remove my mask, wash and dry my hands, and put on a fresh mask. It may seem a little bit overkill to do this, as I am already wearing the mask that I put on when I entered the Hospital, but when you are having chemotherapy treatment, your immune system is severely compromised, so this added step is to protect all of the patients in the unit.

Once I had completed this task, I was introduced to my nurse, Annie. She did her absolute best to put me at rest and explained everything all over again. She told me that I would need to take medications for a few days after each infusion, and checking the list, she dispensed some out of each bottle, giving me a handful of pills with some water to swallow. Popping the open boxes back into the clear bag, she handed it to me and gave me instructions to take it to the satellite pharmacy in the main waiting area, where they would explain which medication to take and when. I photographed the medication list and sent it to Simon; he immediately started researching the side effects.

Here is a list of the medications that I had to take, along with some of the more common side effects.

Ondansetron - one tablet, twice a day -
Headache - Lightheadedness - Dizziness - Drowsiness - Tiredness - Constipation

Dexamethasone - four tablets each morning -
Aggression - Agitation - Anxiety - Decrease in the amount of urine.
Fast, slow, pounding, or irregular heartbeat or pulse - Headache - Mental depression - Mood changes

Metoclopramide - one tablet, three times a day -
Feeling sleepy and a lack of energy - Low mood - Feeling dizzy or faint (low blood pressure) - Diarrhoea
Uncontrollable lip-smacking (Simon found this one rather entertaining, and he couldn't help but message me to inform me)

Omeprazole - one tablet, three times a day -
Back, leg, or stomach pain - Bleeding or crusting sores on the lips - Blisters - Bloody or cloudy urine.
Continuing ulcers or sores in the mouth, Difficulty, burning, or painful urination, or a Frequent urge to urinate.

A general feeling of discomfort or illness.

Filgrastim - injection, starting on day five for five days -
Mild to moderate bone pain - Fever - Diarrhoea - Skin rash -
Weakness

Returning to the unit, Annie asked if I had given any thought to using the 'cold cap'*. I told her I'd decided against it. Then, a patient who had lost her hair came in, and I immediately changed my mind. This decision wasn't made from a stance of vanity but one of fear. I was afraid of losing my hair, which, again, considering everything else, is absolutely ridiculous.

The cold cap is a fluid-filled helmet that fits snugly to your head. It is connected by a tube to a machine that chills and pumps the fluid around. The thought process behind it is that it chills your hair follicles, so the chemotherapy drug doesn't affect them, and you won't lose your hair. I am told that it isn't 100% effective in some cases, but most patients seem to see less hair loss.

Annie switched on the machine, so the liquid began cooling to the correct temperature before it was placed on my head. I retrieved my boredom-busting bits from my bag. These consist of knitting, books, magazines, and adult coloring books, which are full of profanities, so they are right up my street. Thankfully, I also had the foresight to pack a blanket, a cold drink, and some snacks to munch on.

When the cold cap reached the correct temperature, Annie slathered my hair with conditioner; this was to make sure that the cap didn't rip the hair out at the root on removal; yes, the cap really is that snug. I will try my best to describe to you how cold the cap actually is; imagine you are enjoying the heat on some exotic holiday abroad when all of a sudden, someone has snapped their fingers, and you find yourself buried head-first in the Arctic; the temperature difference is that great. I had a brain freeze from the outside in. Each time it felt like my head was gradually getting used to the temperature, I quickly discovered I was wrong. The machine goes through cycles of pump and chill.

The cap naturally warms up because of the temperature of your scalp, but once the fluid in the cap reaches a specific temperature, a fresh lot of chilled fluid is pumped into it. The experience, for me, was an awful one. Especially as you have to wear the cap for 30 minutes before your treatment starts, during your treatment, which is roughly an hour, and then for an hour and a half after your treatment has finished, so the minimum amount of time that you need to wear it for is three hours. I ended up wearing the cap for six hours. The chemotherapy medication is tailor-made each morning for patients, as it is quite costly; they wait for confirmation that the patient has arrived before mixing the necessary chemicals. Due to staffing issues, my medication was delayed in arriving at the unit.

After the third attempt, I am successfully cannulated in readiness for my treatment; I did tell you that I have crappy veins. I was surprised that the chemotherapy nurses are only allowed two attempts at cannulating a patient, so it took two nurses to try to find one of my veins. When speaking with my mum about her chemotherapy treatment previously, she said that her main regret was not having a PICC line when offered one. Because I know how hard it is to find a vein on me, I question whether it might be worth having one fitted for future use. Annie told me they wouldn't rule it out but would see how it goes.

I am hooked up to a saline drip while I wait patiently for the treatment to arrive. Unfortunately, not all of the patients are patient, and some were quite vocal in voicing their disapproval at being made to wait. This created a stressful working environment for their nursing team. I couldn't, and probably never will, understand this mentality. Where on earth could they possibly need to be that is so important that it takes precedence over receiving potentially life-saving treatment?

My infusion finally arrived, and all of a sudden, there was a lot of action and commotion as two nurses checked my details and checked that the infusion was the right one for me. The first three rounds of my treatment consist of two different methods for infusing. Your chemotherapy nurse administers the first part, whilst the second part is administered via an intravenous drip.

Because the first part of the therapy can make you susceptible to mouth ulcers, Annie gives me an ice lolly to suck on as the nurse administers the infusion. The thought process behind the ice lolly is the same theory as that of the cold cap: if the area is chilled, the drug is less likely to affect that part of the body. On the trolley containing my prescribed infusion, next to Annie, are four tubes containing a bright red liquid; I have since learned that this is referred to as 'the Red Devil'. Annie carefully attaches one and slowly presses on the plunger, stopping occasionally so the saline can dilute it before carrying it around my body. Annie informs me that this part of the treatment can make your urine red for a day or so afterwards. I am quite glad they tell you this, although I wasn't expecting this colour change to be instantaneous, so seeing the water at the bottom of the toilet turn bright red immediately following treatment was a bit of a shock.

After Annie administers the fourth syringe of red liquid, I am hooked up to an IV drip for the final part. The IV tube is fed through a machine called a 'pump' before it is connected to my cannula.

Looking around the Chemotherapy Suite, there are approximately 18 chairs for patients to sit in, and they are all occupied. Each patient is either hooked up to a drip like myself, has a chemotherapy nurse administering their treatment, or is waiting for their infusion to arrive.

The treatment unit is a continual revolving door of patients and infusions; each pump trills a set of beeps as the allotted time ends. Sometimes, medication remains, so the nurse sets the machine to another five or ten minutes. Once the bags are emptied of their fluids, the patients are detached from the machines, the cannulas (if they have one) are removed, and they are free to leave. The chairs are then disinfected with new covers put on the pillow that supports your arm during your infusion. Another patient is then called in from the waiting room, and taking their seat, the process starts all over again.

I was completely engrossed in my Ian Rankin novel when my machine began its trill of beeps. I feel a small amount of excitement that I am finished and can go home, completely forgetting that I have to wait for the cold cap therapy to finish as well. My lovely nurse checks the bag, says, 'Oh, I think we can get a bit more out of that,' and sets the machine for another fifteen minutes. So, I am slightly closer to being able to leave, but not as close as I initially thought.

I texted Simon to tell him that I would soon be finished and that he should begin winding down his work, pack his laptop away, and come to the unit so that Annie could show him how to inject me. Although I have been a full-time seamstress for over a decade, and although, during the course of a working day, I would accidentally stab myself repeatedly, I cannot, with the best will in the world, stab myself of my own volition. So, the task of injecting me for five days after each infusion falls to Simon. The injections that I need to have start on day five following the infusion. The medication contained in the syringe is designed to give your immune system, which takes a nosedive on the fifth day, a much-needed boost.

Simon and I are not just husband and wife; we are the best of friends and will do everything we can to support each other as and when required. We always try to see the humour in everything and constantly make fun of each other. We jokingly call this part of my treatment' stabby-stabby' and say that he will be able to tell people that he has stabbed his wife thirty times. Anything to help make light of what we must face for the next nine months.

The machine has beeped its final beep, and I can go home. The cold cap is finally removed and the relief on my scalp after its removal feels fantastic. I swear that my head has shrunk to the size of a pin, just like a character from the film Beetlejuice.

I'm unsure how I expected to feel immediately following my

infusion. But I walk out of the hospital hand in hand with Simon, a bag of prescription medications tucked underneath my arm, and I feel absolutely fine. Pulling out of the hospital car park, I make the round-robin of calls and texts. After a while, you are just fed up with talking about it, and you begin to feel like a record stuck on repeat where everyone asks the same questions.

I am amazed that I feel fine--absolutely fine. I didn't have any of the side effects that they said I would get. I began thinking, 'This is going to be a breeze. I can continue to work. I am obviously one of the lucky ones, and it won't affect me that much.' Oh, how wrong I was.

I went shopping with my daughter on the Wednesday immediately following my treatment. The mask was a permanent feature, which caused a few people to stare; they probably thought, 'Sheep!' But all of the staff at the Hospital had repeated over and over about wearing a mask because of my weakened immunity. So that is precisely what I will do. It was lovely spending some quality time with Rach; it is something that we haven't really done since before her teenage years, which is about the time that she became satan incarnate. Luckily, we laugh about it all now, and she is one of my best friends. So, parents of teenagers who are testing you daily, stick with it, and hopefully, they will become wonderful human beings who you will be continually proud of. I know I am.

Waking on Thursday morning, I swear that I felt like a fleet of HGVs had run over me; every single bone in my body throbbed. My head was pounding, and my mouth was dryer than the Sahara desert. I felt awful! But I still made the effort and got out of bed, put on my newly purchased pyjamas and settled on the sofa to watch a film. It is a film I didn't watch, not because it was rubbish and not worth watching, but because I fell asleep; I only woke up when I heard Harrison arriving home from school. So I had slept the whole day and was still exhausted.

The look of glee on Simon's face, along with the words' it's stabby-stabby time' when I woke on Friday, really made me chuckle. He was clearly looking forward to this. Wipe, stab, plunge, done. It's quite simple really, and took it less than a minute, but I still cried. I'm not scared of needles, not in the slightest. I cried because I felt that the dealer had dealt a shit hand and that it wasn't fair that Simon was having to do this. Although he made light of it, I am sure that this wasn't really a task he wanted to do or was relishing in.

Top tip: Ensure you have enough activities to keep you occupied. I took small knitting projects, adult colouring books, novels to read, my Kindle, and plenty of games on my phone. I also packed some snacks and drinks.

FIRST HOSPITAL ADMISSION

22nd October 2022
Despite spending most of the day asleep, I heard my bed calling me a lot earlier than I would have usually climbed into it. I dutifully obeyed, falling fast asleep almost as soon as my head hit the pillow. I slept so deeply that I didn't hear Simon come to bed, which in itself is unusual, as, in the past, I have likened him to a bull elephant on a rampage. But when I woke in the small hours, I instantly knew that he was there.

I don't know what woke me up, but I felt awful. I can't even begin to tell you which part of me felt awful, as I honestly didn't know. All I did know was that I just felt worse than I can ever remember in my life. I lay awake, trying to work out what to do, when he switched on his bedside light with a 'Are you ok?'

I told him I felt awful, and he immediately grabbed the thermometer, taking my temperature; we saw that it was slightly higher than the temperature printed on our oncologist's advice card. So we followed the advice, and Simon called the 24-hour helpline. Listening to the one-sided conversation, I ascertained that I had to go to the Hospital. We quickly threw on some clothes, woke Harrison to tell him what had happened, and informed him that the Hospital had advised us to go and see the medical team. Then, we bundle ourselves into the car with a book each and head to Bath.

There was more traffic on the road than I was expecting. Admittedly, the bulk of it was taxis, no doubt taking the last dregs of revellers home after a night of drinking and dancing.

Post-COVID in the UK saw a massive strain on the National Health Service; there was a shortage of medical professionals, which had a knock-on effect on all departments at the Hospital. This caused a backlog at the Accident and Emergency Department, forcing ambulances with their patients onboard to wait at the side of the road until there was room to drive around to the drop-off zone, unload their patients and then head to the next emergency. Covid, apparently, was still causing problems, as there were rarely any free beds on the wards. Patients would have to wait in Accident and Emergency after their initial assessment for a bed to become available if they would be admitted.

The nurse who took Simon's call to the 24-hour helpline told us to go to the Medical Assessment Unit (MAU), but after pressing the buzzer and waiting patiently with nothing happening, we headed next door to A&E. It was overflowing, with every seat having a bottom firmly plopped in it, and standing room only. Some people are holding various parts of their bodies, alongside others in various states of drunkenness. We head straight to the reception desk and tell them that we have been told to go to MAU but haven't been able to raise anyone there. One of the nurses takes us to the unit, buzzes us in and tells the nurse on duty why we are there.

She had obviously been expecting us as she approached, saying, 'Lisa?' I then confirmed my date of birth and showed her the card with my hospital number. I now know this number off by heart; due to needing to repeat it so often, it has been burnt into my brain.

I follow the nurse to a curtained cubicle containing an A&E trolley (it's a bed, but one of the most uncomfortable beds possible. They are typically only used for a short while to assess or treat a patient, before moving them to a ward, or discharging them). A patient identity bracelet is put on my wrist before she cannulates me. On each of my hospital admissions, this was the standard procedure until I had a PICC line fitted. The nurse took some blood for testing, along with my temperature, blood pressure, and blood oxygen level.

I am hooked up to a bag of saline to stop the cannula from drying out whilst waiting for the IV antibiotics to arrive. Whilst undergoing chemotherapy treatment, your immune system is seriously compromised, so if any patient who is undergoing treatment is admitted with an elevated temperature, antibiotics are administered before any blood results are returned as a matter of protocol.

It is the middle of the night. Nurses whisper in hushed tones as they go about their business of caring for the other patients on the unit. Simon and I sit in absolute silence, hoping to hear my name on one of the nurses' lips and hoping for a clue as to whether or not I will be going home.

We hear footsteps approaching our cubicle before the curtain is whipped back and a very young-looking doctor enters (they all appear young if I'm honest, but it's probably because I am getting older). 'Well, Mrs Holman (which only serves to make me feel even older), it's looking like an infection. But we don't know where, so you're staying with us for now. We'll try to find you a more comfortable bed on one of the wards, but they are in short supply, so this might not be possible. Any questions?'

I'll admit to being slightly dumbfounded. How did I end up here? Simon spoke before me, 'So, is Lisa staying overnight?'
'Yes, possibly for a few nights. We need to get this infection under control. If you don't already have one with you, can you get her an overnight bag?'

We don't have an overnight bag either with us or packed at home, and suddenly, I feel very disorganised. Simon confirms that he'll head home and sort a bag out for me, and I am in tears; I do not want to be here. I want to be at home, snuggled in my own bed, with my own creature comforts around me. I do not want to listen to the raspy breathing of the poor patient lying in the bed next to mine. Subconsciously, I find myself dutifully listening for each inhale and exhale, trying to quell the rising panic if there is even the briefest of pauses in case the breathing stops entirely. However, I am unsure what the actual protocol would be should this arise. Do I ring my bell? Or theirs? Or shout really loudly whilst flapping my arms around like a stranded pigeon?

Simon does his best to console me, promising to return with supplies in a couple of hours. In my stupidity, I came to the Hospital, fully clothed in Jeans and a jumper; a hospital gown was offered to me, which I quickly refused because that meant I was staying, right? After Simon leaves, I climb onto the bed and make myself as comfortable as possible. Whilst continuing to listen to 'raspy breath', there was the unmistakably rhythmic beep of a heart monitor drifting up from further down the ward.

I must have somehow gained comfort from these alien sounds and drifted off to sleep. It felt like I had just closed my eyes when a nurse awoke me; my antibiotics were here. I watched as the saline drip was removed from the stand and the nurse put antibiotics in their place. The way all the parts fit together seamlessly reminded me slightly of Meccano: unscrew that bit, put that bit on there and re-screw. This may sound strange, but I could smell the antibiotics; they have a weird chemical smell, and if I breathed too deeply, it would sting my eyes. Taking short breaths only, I manage to drift off to sleep again.

I discovered that the mornings in the Hospital start early, as I wake up to the cheery sound of 'tea or coffee' followed by the squeaky wheels of the metal tea trolley as they push it from one patient to another. As soon as the drinks are dispensed, the breakfast trolley is wheeled around; cereals, porridge and toast are available. Knowing that I need to eat, even though I have no appetite, I make my choice and settle on the hard trolley that is currently my bed to eat it.

I phone Simon whilst I eat, eager for him to come back and keep me company, whilst secretly hoping that he will go along with my plan and allow me to discharge myself; I know that he won't, but having a plan doesn't do any harm, does it?. He told me that he needed to email work to let them know what was happening and to arrange some time off before he could pack my bag and return. My heart sinks to my stomach with the knowledge that he won't return for a while yet and the fact that I want to go home.

I lay back on the bed, trying to get as comfortable as possible. If

I am being truthful, the MAU beds aren't really beds; they are A&E trolleys. The 'mattress', if we want to call it that, is as hard as a rock, and the pillows are wafer-thin. So, whilst I do not want to be here, I hope a bed will become available in a ward, as I am sure it would be much more comfortable than the one I currently occupy.

I am bored, and I am scared. Luckily, my phone is fully charged, and I have plenty of puzzle games to keep me occupied. However, due to being scared, I am unable to concentrate on them. As an adult, I have always been the sort of person who goes a million miles an hour, always busy, busy. Even when sat in the evenings I would be knitting or doing a cross-stitch. Sometimes, I would have my laptop in front of me and use the time to do administrative work for my sewing business. I will, however, admit that as a child, if I could find a way to sit and watch television all day, I would, much to my parent's disgust.

My phone begins ringing, and it is my Dad, asking how I am and that Simon has phoned everyone to let them know what has happened. I can't help but cry on the phone, which upsets my Dad, something that I would never do intentionally. I quickly pull myself together, get my emotions in check, and manage to have a conversation with him, telling him that I don't know how long I'll be in. He offered to come up and see me, but I told him that it would be pointless as I might be home later. Actually, looking back, my Dad offered to come up each time I was admitted to the Hospital. I never took him up on this though.

As soon as I finished talking to my Dad, my mum, my sister Joanne, Rachael and Tash called me. I felt sorry for 'raspy breath' and 'beepy machine' as I was making more noise than them with the amount of phone calls I was taking, especially if I laughed (I have quite a loud laugh years ago our family nearly got asked to leave a Chinese restaurant because of the amount of noise that we were making)

I let my paranormal friends know in the 'bean-faced b**tard' chat group. Karin called me straight away and made me laugh by insulting me again. The rest of the group sent me messages, jokes and inappropriate memes, which made me chuckle when I opened them.

Simons back! Yay, he's here! My spirits were lifted instantaneously when I saw him walk into my cubicle. In one hand, he had an overnight bag, packed with the help of a phone call to Rachael, and in the other, he had a carrier bag with magazines and snacks. He's such a good egg; yes, at times, he could annoy me to the point of me wanting to commit murder and then bury him underneath the patio. I am sure a lot of marriages and longstanding partnerships are the same. But, despite this, I love him entirely; he is my soulmate and best friend, rolled into one fantastic human being.

I was correct in thinking that he wouldn't let me discharge myself. The raised 'really?' eyebrow said it all. We talked of all the plans we have for when I am better: doing our motorbike tests and getting a motorbike each. Then, touring on them, first around the UK and then touring further afield, including Europe and Route 66 in the States. When my lunch arrives, he disappears to the restaurant to get something to eat himself, promising that he won't be long.

Instantly, my fear returned, and I honestly didn't know what was causing it. My heart feels like it is about to explode, and, despite being and remaining positive, the constant 'What if..?' questions circulate in my head; 'What if I have to stay here for a while?' 'What if I have chosen the wrong course of treatment?" What if I don't make it?' The whole way through my treatment, several times a day, the last two questions would circulate round and round in my head. Occasionally, even now, a year on, the questions surface from time to time, and speaking with other cancer survivors, these thoughts may never leave me.

I can hear the doctor doing his rounds. With my fingers crossed, I repeat the mantra, 'Please let me go home... please let me go home...'. A nurse comes in and does my observations again: blood pressure, blood oxygen, temperature, and heart rate.

Apparently, my temperature is still elevated, so I will need to stay another night to give the antibiotics time to work. Another bag is put on the stand, and I am attached to it through the cannula in my hand.

Simon looks exhausted; like me, he has probably had little sleep. He tells me he needs to go home, one to make dinner for Harrison and check that he is ok, and two to catch up on some much-needed sleep. For selfish reasons alone, I want him to stay. But I know he is spinning many plates, so I don't say anything. A quick peck on the cheek as a goodbye, and I watch as he walks towards the ward exit; as he reaches the door, he turns and quickly waves goodbye. He undoubtedly harbours the same feelings as me, although neither of us voices them.

So I am alone again, but luckily I have some magazines to read. Hopefully, I will be able to submerge myself into other people's lives and give myself a little break from my overwhelming reality. The magazines did little to distract me. I found myself struggling to concentrate on the words that were swimming on the brightly edited pages. After reading the same paragraph several times, I gave up and tried to catch up on some sleep instead. New antibiotics were hooked up every six hours, with my observations being done more frequently than that, so I have been starved of sleep throughout the night and am feeling quite tired.

Night turns to day again, and I am still on the concrete trolley; my back feels like it is about to break in half. The welcoming sound of 'Tea or Coffee Love' as the volunteers go about their rounds, then here comes the breakfast trolley. I still don't really feel like eating; my stomach aches and feels like it has lead weights in it (it has been like this since my diagnosis, and despite trying to have a positive mental attitude, my stomach will not play ball). Still, I know that I must eat or I may never get well enough to go home.

After breakfast, I stood at the end of my bed, looking down the ward towards the door that Simon would walk through. I found myself rocking from one foot to the other, pointing and flexing my toes before rocking to the other foot. It's strange how therapeutic I found this simple thing. It gave me something to concentrate on: rock, point, flex, rock, point, flex, etc.

I spotted a doctor heading my way. He looked surprised to see me rocking while staring into space. Coming to a stop just in front of me, 'Lisa?'

Replying with 'Yes', I quickly scoot back to my bed so the doctor can come into my cubicle and draw the curtain. It always makes me chuckle internally when they pull the curtain for 'privacy' when everyone can hear every word that is being said.

'Great news, the antibiotics have started to work, and your temperature has been brought down sufficiently enough for you to be able to go home. You will be discharged with oral antibiotics to take for the next five days.'

The excitement and joy bubbled up from below, and I honestly could have hugged him. I beamed,' So I can go home?'

'Yes, you can go home as soon as the pharmacy has delivered your prescription. I must warn you that sometimes it can be an hour or more. So if you need to phone anyone to collect you, you can do that now.'

'Ok, thank you so much, and thank you for taking such great care of me.'

I'm going home, I'm going home, Lisa's going home!

I phone Simon to tell him the good news, but he doesn't answer, which means that he is either still asleep, his phone is on silent, he has lost it, or he is on his way but has left his phone at home. I left him a message regardless and phoned Rachael and Harrison to see if they could have any better luck raising him. He seems to spend most of his time trying to find his phone, wallet or keys, which, as you can imagine, opens him up for much ridicule in our house.

It took an age for Simon to arrive. But even when he did, we could not leave as my prescription hadn't yet been delivered. The hospital pharmacy must have been extremely busy, as it felt as if we were waiting hours for my medication to arrive.

Simon made himself busy by packing everything up and taking it to the car so that when the medication arrived, we just needed to walk to the car without being burdened with baggage. No doubt he would have taken a quick detour to the Hospital Restaurant, in the hopes that they were serving Chilli-con-carne. For some reason, he seemed to like the food they served. I, for one, cannot stand it, but I suppose I have been put off because of the sheer amount of admissions I have had.

It appeared that I was not the only patient being released, as I heard the nurse talking with another patient about their prescription. I wait patiently for the nurse to bring mine so that I can go home. Playing games on your phone is an excellent way to distract yourself and kill some time because it felt like I had only just started looking at my phone when the nurse appeared around the corner with my antibiotics. She pulled them out of the brown paper bag and explained the dosage and when to take them, also reminding me that if at any point I felt unwell, I should call the 24-hour oncology helpline.

You cannot believe my eagerness to go home, but I wait patiently for Simon to return. There is absolutely no point in me trying to find my way to the restaurant or the main car park as I have no sense of direction. I always joke that I could get lost in a brown paper bag, even with directions. So, waiting patiently is my only option.

As soon as he arrived, I jumped off the bed, and he hugged me tightly; he was as eager as me to go home. Cancer affects everyone, not just the patient but anyone who knows and cares about them. I sometimes think that, in some ways, it affects their immediate family more than the patient.

We walk hand in hand back to the car, discussing what to do when we get home. I decide that I am going straight to bed as I am exhausted. Simon told me that he would join me and watch the TV quietly. I think that he wants to be close to me and keep an eye on me in case I take a downward turn.

I fell asleep as soon as my head hit the pillow. Every now and then, I would hear the beep of the temperature gun as Simon checked on me. He took such good care of me, waking me when I had to take my meds and checking my temperature constantly, which makes me think that perhaps he has researched how bad an infection can be for a cancer patient.

After I recovered, I decided to batten down the hatches. I only saw a select number of people; they were made to take a COVID test before visiting, and if they felt unwell in any way at all, even just something as mundane as a sniffly nose, we would ask them to steer clear. Even after we let them in, they weren't allowed to get close to me and had to wear a mask for the entirety of their visit. I avoided large public places, and most of our shopping was delivered. It felt like we were in the first COVID lockdown again; anything that came into the house would be wiped with antibacterial wipes. We were super careful to make sure that the environment was as sterile as possible; we were doing everything that we could to make sure that I wasn't hospitalised again.

Top tip: Always have an overnight bag in your car; you never know when you will be admitted, so at least your first night will be comfortable. Don't forget to take your phone charger.

ONCOLOGY APPOINTMENT

2nd November 2022
I'm bricking it! Despite being told that this was a routine appointment, the little niggling voice in the back of my head would not leave me be. 'It has spread ...', 'It is too late ...', 'There is nothing they can do ...' constantly whirring around inside my head like a stuck record, or your least favourite song, stuck on repeat with no option to change the track, or turn the volume down.

What didn't help was being kept waiting. I'd estimate that we were waiting for about two hours. I know that appointments can run over, but despite knowing this, it doesn't help you mentally.

We were called to the secondary waiting area, which consisted of chairs lined up along the wall, with the oncologists' office doors opposite them - the layout made me feel like I was a naughty student waiting to be seen by the headmaster. One by one, we watched as couples were called into an office before leaving to go home. We were the last ones seen, which did nothing to quell the rising tide of panic within me.

I had assumed that I would be seeing the same oncologist assigned to me on my first appointment, but I didn't, and to this day, I haven't seen her since. Yes, the NHS was in a state of turmoil at the time, still suffering from the aftereffects of COVID-19 and trying to make a recovery. With many medical professionals leaving, they were understaffed, and the remaining staff were underpaid, which meant there were strikes across the UK. But I still maintain that if I had seen the same oncologist each time, my drastic decline would have been picked up on, and I may not still be suffering from the side effects of the severe reaction I had during treatment. As you continue to read through this journal, you will have an understanding of how deeply I was affected and how drastically I declined. If anything, I think this needs to be addressed and changed.

The oncologist I saw was very professional. She had a student oncologist in the room with her and asked if I had any objections to her staying. I firmly believe that medical students must also learn how to interact with patients while studying. There is only so much that can be learnt from a book, so I, of course, gave my permission for her to stay.

We reviewed my medication and the side effects that I had suffered so far. I mentioned the hospital stay, which she was surprised by, so she clearly hadn't read all of my notes. She said that it was nothing to be concerned about and that these things sometimes happen, so providing that my blood results came back as okay, the treatment would continue as planned for the following Monday.

I would have liked to have discussed in more detail what we could do to ensure this doesn't happen again, but we were dismissed quite quickly. It felt as if they were eager to get home themselves. We gathered our belongings and made our way back to the car park. Walking through the hospital at this time of night was eerily quiet; the throng of people in the atrium that you would typically need to navigate past was no more, possibly because the cafe, pharmacy and friend's shop were now closed. Except for a few stragglers seated at the tables who had made use of the vending machines close by, the hospital felt empty; you could almost hear a pin drop.

As we made our way home, the sky was already pitch black, and the heavy downpour that had been forecast was throwing rain at us as we drove. I made the round-robin of phone calls and text messages, telling everyone I was okay and what was discussed. I posted on the BFB message page telling them that we were on our way home and I was fine, to responses of thumbs up, insults, and memes.

BRAVING THE SHAVE

After deciding that there was absolutely no way that I could continue with the cold cap treatment, I opted to get a wig so that when I go out and about, people won't stare as much, and hopefully, fingers crossed, I will feel halfway normal. I made an appointment with the 'wig lady' who was recommended by my breast nurse (each breast cancer patient is allotted a dedicated nurse to contact if they have any questions).

The oncology department has been very well thought out. As well as having a consultation room for the Macmillan charity, that houses a dedicated support team offering help and advice to patients and their families, there is also a satellite pharmacy so that patients can discuss their medications without being within hearing distance of the crowds of people that pass the main pharmacy in the atrium. Next to the Macmillan office is a little room with a door sign stating that it is the 'Hairdresser'. It isn't really a hairdressers, as that would just be too cruel, but this is where the wig lady sets up shop one day a week. I suppose in calling the room the hairdressers, they are trying to normalise the wearing of wigs, and it helps the patients feel like their appearance hasn't changed and gives them something to look forward to. They even have a little waiting area, with magazines containing pictures of all the different wigs that can be purchased.

A month or so before being diagnosed, I had taken the plunge and dyed my boring brown hair. I had it changed into a gorgeous bright purple and pink, and I absolutely loved it. Even though these colours don't stay in your hair for long and fade with each wash, it was amazing when it was at its most vibrant. As I loved my bright hair so much, I thought that I could get a really funky and bright wig.

Rachael wanted to take me to this appointment; she hadn't been able to take me to any so far, so it was lovely that she came to this one. It was a bit like a 'girly day out'. As she doesn't live round the corner, she had to drive nearly an hour to collect me and then the 30-45 minutes to the hospital. Then she dropped me home afterwards before going home, so she spent a lot of time driving.

We arrived early, which is always lovely. Despite being late for most things, since being diagnosed, the thought of being late for something made me feel physically sick. We grabbed a takeout coffee and made our way to the oncology department. Signing in at reception, we settled in the waiting area and looked through the magazines of available wigs. To my disappointment, there were no funky ones with bright colours; they all looked amazing and very realistic, but they were all in natural colours. My hair was naturally brunette, so I decided that if a funky colour was not available, I might as well choose a colour that wasn't my natural one, so I opted to look at the blonde ones that were on offer.

The 'hairdresser', who was called either Julie or Linda, for argument's sake, we'll call her Julie, ushered us into a small room. A chair was at the far end for the patient's guest, and one was for the patient, who was set in front of a tabletop mirror. I took my seat and was an absolute bag of nerves. I had only ever worn a wig once, and that was for an 80s fancy dress party; I went as a punk rocker and donned a black and fluorescent pink mohican wig. So, sitting in the room piled high with boxes of various sizes, having to decide on the wig that would become part of my attire was nerve-racking. I thumbed through the magazines and showed Julie the ones I found myself most drawn to. They were all shades of blonde and long, longer than my natural hair had been since having my daughter nearly thirty years ago. I tried them all on and hated each and every one of them. In the end, because she could sense how downhearted I was beginning to feel, Julie made some suggestions and began to pull out boxes that she felt would suit me better. She was a true professional and worth her weight in gold; she was absolutely spot on! The wig I chose looked more like my current hairstyle and colour; now that the bright colours had washed out, it was more of a blonde. Putting the wig on and looking in the mirror, I looked like me. The wig was so well made that you would have thought it was my natural hair. Because of the retail cost of the wig, I had to pay a bit extra as the NHS prescription is only valid for a specific price. I also bought the stand and the special shampoo and conditioning treatments. So determined was I to lead as normal a life as possible whilst going through my treatment. I envisioned lunches with friends, shopping for baby bits with Rachael, going on cinema trips, etc. Unfortunately, though, none of this actually happened.

Top tip: Do not buy a wig cap. It makes you look like Golem from Lord of the Rings, and they are incredibly tight. It feels as if your brain is going to pop out of the top of your head.

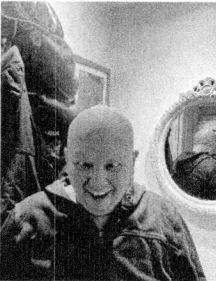

KEEPING MYSELF BUSY

I have always been the type of person to hit the day running in adult life anyway; as a teenager, I would have been more than happy to spend the entire day cocooned in my bed.

After completing the last pair of curtains that I had already started before diagnosis, I called all of my remaining clients to tell them that I was no longer able to complete their orders and that I no longer had any sewing to do. I had to find something that would occupy my mind, or I would have gone stir-crazy. Rachael, the ever-thoughtful daughter that she is, bought me a beautiful piece of diamond art; it pictured a beach scene with a sunset and 'Love' written in pebbles. I had never done one of these before, but I knew that my Mum and sister loved doing them. Rachael and I sat at the kitchen table, taking turns to do a bit each. I really enjoyed it, and it is something that I still do today.

I would spend a few hours each day sticking bits of plastic onto a preprinted sheet whilst watching a program on my phone at the same time, just in case my mind would wander and turn to dark thoughts. Looking back, I realise how much time I actually spent doing this as I watched all of the seasons of Game Of Thrones, Angel, Buffy the Vampire Slayer, and The Crown. So this gives you an idea of how much time I spent sitting at the kitchen table. I am not going to lie; it really is quite addictive.

Luckily, it isn't mentally taxing at all, as the treatment had already begun to have an effect on my cognitive ability. At times, I struggled to form a sentence; if I could create one, you can guarantee that I would forget it almost as soon as I begin to speak. Trying to remember the simplest of things was beyond me. Even the names of everyday items, such as toothbrushes, soap, cups, etc., would evade me. My 'brain' has started to reappear in small increments, but I am still a long way from where I used to be and what I used to be capable of. You have no idea how long it has taken for me to write and finish this book.

The diamond art helped to take my mind off of whatever it was trying to fixate on; usually, these fixations would centre around extremely dark thoughts; at one point, I was even trying to decide what type of coffin I would like. If you are interested, it was the cheapest one, and if adding pink glitter was an option, that is the one I would pick.

For anyone unfortunate enough to suffer from mental health and/or anxiety issues, I would highly recommend taking up a craft such as diamond art as a way of self-help.

The two paragraphs above were originally written as follows;
The diamond art helped to take my mind off of whatever it was trying to fixate on; usually, these fixations would centre around extremely dark thoughts; at one point, I was even trying to decide what type of coffin I would like. If you are interested, it was the cheapest one, and if adding pink glitter was an option, that is the one I would pick. I would highly recommend it as a way of self-help for those who are unfortunate enough to suffer from mental health and anxiety issues.
Which caused raucous laughter when Sarah and I were proofing it together.

GOODBYE TO MY HAIR

5th November 2022

As I had decided that I wasn't going to use the cold-cap treatment again, and because I didn't want to wake up each morning with clumps of my long hair on the pillow, I had made an appointment with Cara, my hairdresser and Rachael's friend, to cut my hair off the day before my second chemotherapy. I wanted to keep my long hair intact for as long as possible. I knew this would be very hard to do, but it was the lesser of two evils.

Unfortunately, Cara was ill and unable to come to my house to do it, so she gave Rachael instructions on how to do it. So I sat in the middle of my kitchen whilst she set to work. After partitioning my hair into more manageable pieces and securing them with hairbands, she began to cut my hair. The sound of the scissors cutting through strands of my hair brought on floods of tears, and try as I might, I could not stop sobbing uncontrollably. Rachael would occasionally stop and kiss my head, telling me that it was alright, it would grow back, and she'd do a good job and try not to cut an ear off. Next came the clippers, a number 2 all over, and I was absolutely devastated, watching as my hair fell to the floor around me.

It was a strange feeling. I knew that it was the best option in the long run, but the heartbreak that I felt was almost like the feeling of grief when you lose a loved one.

After Rachael had finished cutting my hair, Simon said, 'Come on then, let's do me' It was a gesture that meant the world and was completely unexpected. I was overcome with emotion, and I couldn't help but cry as I watched his hair being shaved (he had a number one all over, so incredibly short)

Despite telling a few select friends, I hadn't made my diagnosis public. Not because I wanted to keep it a secret but because I didn't want people's sympathy or to be the cause of their worrying. But after having my hair cut, I pulled on my big girl knickers and donned the 'F@@K Breast Cancer' T-shirt that my friend Amie had bought me. Rachael took a photo of first me on my own first, with thumbs up whilst trying desperately to hide the tears and then one with Simon. I then made a public Facebook* post, announcing to the world that I had just become a statistic. The outpouring of love, support and sympathy was overwhelming; in the end, I had to silence my phone. It was becoming too much to bear.

FACEBOOK POST

I have been pondering for some time about whether to go public with this or not. Then I realised that keeping things a secret does nothing to raise awareness.

On 29th September I was diagnosed with Breast Cancer. I have already started my course of 6 chemotherapy sessions spaced 3 weeks apart. I have so many tablets to take to combat the numerous side effects, I honestly swear that I rattle when I walk.

The reason for this post is not to gain sympathy, it doesn't help and just makes me sad. The reason I've decided to make this public is to raise awareness, if this post reminds just one of you to check your breasts, it's worth it. And gents, don't think that you are immune to this awful disease, whether you are built like Jason Momoa (yes please), or have man boobs that could feature in the Guinness World Records, check yourself, please.

Much love, Lisa xx

MY AMAZING HUSBAND - SIMON

Sensing the downward spiral of my mental health, Simon did the most amazing thing. He disappeared for half an hour; I didn't think anything of it and didn't question where he was. When he returned to the lounge, I saw that he had shaved his head completely bald; no hair was left! I was utterly shocked and so overwhelmed with emotion that I began to cry, again.

For whatever reason, possibly because she is old and senile, our lovely cat 'Ogie' would perch on the back of the sofa behind Simon and lick his bald head. If Simon were to 'forcibly' remove her, she would return to where she was sitting and continue where she left off. I can only imagine what it must have felt like, a cat's sandpapery tongue licking your bald head, but the look on Simons's face left me with no confusion as to the fact that it wasn't enjoyable! All I could do was sit and laugh as Simon would wrinkle up his face each time her tongue came into contact with his head.

Around this time, my step-mum, Sue, video-called me. When I answered, I saw that she had also clipped her hair as a symbol of support for me. She kept clipping it as soon as it began to grow through my entire chemotherapy treatment. We both agreed that it was the wrong time of year to lose one's hair.

After I made a post on Facebook (they were few and far between) about it really being the wrong time of year to be bald, my lovely friend Maxine knitted me a bobble hat, which became referred to as my daytime hat. The one my Mum knitted me (sans bobble) became my nighttime hat. I was rarely seen without a hat on, as whenever I didn't wear one, I became extremely cold extremely quickly.

SECOND CHEMOTHERAPY TREATMENT

7th November 2022

I would like to say that, as I now knew what to expect, I felt a lot calmer, but unfortunately, I cannot make this claim.

I have never suffered from anxiety before, and until you have, you cannot really appreciate how it affects you and how it can impact your everyday life. For me, it felt as if I was about to have a heart attack, and my heart would explode out of my chest wall, like something from one of the Alien films, covering everyone within a radius of a few feet with blood and guts.

Arriving at the Hospital, Simon dropped me off directly outside before parking the car. This is because not only was I starting to become extremely weak, but we only had minutes to spare before my appointment. I walked slowly to the oncology department, immediately took a wrong turn, and got lost again. Luckily, Simon wasn't far behind me. He telephoned me when he saw that I wasn't on the ward and then came to find me before leading me to the correct waiting room.

After following their strict handwashing and mask rules, I settled into my chair on the chemotherapy unit. Again, unpacking my boredom busters before one of the nurses tried and failed to cannulate me. They must have a file somewhere on difficult patients; in my case, it would have been because of my veins. In an attempt to coax my veins to the surface, my hands were dumped into a bucket of warm water, with strict instructions not to remove them. After about 10 minutes, the nurse returned, removed my hands from the bucket, and wrapped each in a towel.

She had an amazing Caribbean accent: 'I do this one, sit on the other.' So, with my hand wrapped in a towel, I obeyed and sat on it. Cannula numbers three and four also failed, so another nurse came for attempts five and six. I must admit that now I was beginning to panic a little, and I started counting all of the nurses that were on the ward, worrying about what would happen if they ran out of people. Luckily, attempt number five worked, and I was now successfully cannulated.

Again, my treatment was delayed, but I'm not worried. I have plenty of things to keep me occupied, and a nurse has shown me that my chair reclines--how fantastic!

My infusion finally arrived after lunch, and it was the same procedure as before. I confirmed my full name and date of birth, and two nurses independently checked that it was indeed the right treatment for me before beginning the infusion.

The nurse reminded me that I needed to collect my Filgastrim before leaving as it had to be refrigerated. I asked Annie if it was worth exploring having a PICC line installed, and she told me that she had already spoken with the department and they should be in touch soon with an appointment. I didn't really know what a PICC line was; I just knew that if it removed the number of times that the nurses had to stab me, thus eliminating the number of bruises on me and stress on them, then it had to be worth having done. No one explained in detail what was involved in having one either, merely that a tube was inserted into your arm to make the treatment easier. I'll go into more detail later so that you have all of the information just in case you ever find yourself in the same situation.

Once my treatment had finished, I left the oncology department, looking for Simon; he wasn't in his usual position in the waiting room. So I quickly called him as I walked towards the restaurant, almost sure that he was filling his face. He answered quickly and told me that he had walked into the town centre, about a 20-30 minute walk. I tell him that I have finished treatment, and he says that he will make his way back and for me to wait in the oncology waiting area. But my anxiety wouldn't let me go back; people would stare at me; they probably wouldn't, but my mind would not accept this. So I ordered a coffee and muffin and sat in the cafe in the main foyer. I don't know why I ordered them; I had no intention of eating or drinking any of them. I suppose it is because it is what is expected of you. The nausea had already started, and the thought of putting anything in my mouth made me want to be sick. I sat in my chair, head firmly hung as low as possible, just in case someone looked at me and recognised me as a cancer patient rather than Lisa. Sitting in a cafe, surrounded by people, hoping that no one would notice that I hadn't touched a drop of coffee and that all I had done to the muffin was break it into ever-decreasing pieces, made my anxiety hit the roof. If anyone got too close or if there was a loud noise in the vicinity, I would jump out of my skin. I absolutely hated being like this, but it was something that I had no control over at all.

Simon finally arrives and we walk back to the car together, with him supporting me as much as he is able to. Climbing into the car, I sit back and make the round-robin phone calls, trying desperately not to vomit due to the nausea being so bad.

When I arrived home, I went straight to bed. Exhaustion made sleeping difficult, but I felt so much more relaxed at home. I put on some mind-numbing television, knowing that if I did manage to snooze, I wouldn't be annoyed at myself for missing a crucial part of the storyline.

The following days passed in a daze. I knew that I would get up each morning, shower if I had the energy, or throw on some clean pyjamas and settle downstairs on the sofa. Each time, I would generally fall asleep, and each time when I woke, it would be evident that Simon had popped in to check on me as I would be covered with a blanket or three.

'It's 'stabby-stabby' day'. Again, the look of pure glee on Simon's face makes me laugh. I honestly believe that laughter is the best remedy; it really does lift your spirits. So Simon and I did our best to find something to laugh about every day. Obviously, on' stabby-stabby' days, this was made so much easier.

Each time a letter came from the hospital, I would begin to panic and feel sick with worry, the constant questions of 'what if it's spread?' 'Have I chosen the right route for my treatment?' 'Am I going to die?' 'Are they telling me everything?' would be on repeat like the needle of a record player jumping in a too-deep groove on the record. This morning was no different when two letters came from the hospital, the telltale blue' NHS' logo clearly displayed across the top of the envelope.

'You open it, I can't look.' Not that I'm burying my head in the sand, but the medication has caused brain fog, and nothing makes sense to me. It could have been something relatively simple like a change of appointment, but the way my mind was working against me at this time, I doubt that it would have allowed me to understand the content of the letters.

'OK, so you have two appointments, luckily they are on the same day. One is for your ultrasound at the Breast Unit, and the other is for your PICC line.'

Phew, instant relief; I can breathe again.

Top tip: Focus on the future. What are you going to do when the treatment has finished? Make lots of plans, whether it be to visit friends or travel the world.

SECOND HOSPITAL ADMISSION

16th November 2022
I've got COVID-19. I couldn't believe it; we had been so careful. Anti-baking everything that came in the house and screening everyone for COVID before we would let them in. How on earth could I have caught it? I don't go out anymore; the fear and anxiety that I experienced were so bad that I couldn't even contemplate leaving the sanctuary of my home. The only place I had been was the hospital, so it stands to reason that this is where I must have come into contact with it.

My temperature was through the roof, so after calling the 24-hour helpline, they advised me to go to the hospital to get checked, just in case there was another infection.

We wouldn't be caught out this time; we grabbed my boredom-busting bag and an overnight case and drove to the hospital. As there wasn't any room in the Medical Assessment Unit, I was admitted to A&E; all of my observations were taken, and after being successfully cannulated and having quite a few vials of blood taken, I can't recall how many times it took to cannulate me, as I was in a complete daze.

However, I do recall asking for more blankets because I was freezing even though my temperature was through the roof, and you could have fried an egg on my forehead!

I like to think of myself as a compassionate person; I want to believe that people are ordinarily good; there are just the occasional ones whose morals and ethics may not align with yours. I always try to see the good in everyone and see things from both sides if there is a disagreement. Because I try not to inconvenience people or cause them to worry, I kept my mask on the entire time I was around them to protect others just in case I had COVID-19 (I wasn't aware at this time) and also to protect myself as my immune system was still dangerously low. The gentleman in the bed opposite me buzzed a nurse, looking at me whilst he spoke to her; she then came across and drew my curtain. Others may have had an issue with this, but I found it quite funny. We all have to do what we feel is best to protect ourselves. There is no right or wrong for how each individual deals with the same or a similar thing, and we shouldn't cast judgment on or ridicule those who do not respond in the same way as ourselves.

Sometime later, a hospital porter pulled back my curtain, and he wheeled me to the X-ray department for the obligatory chest X-ray, which always seemed to happen whenever I came to the hospital with a suspected infection. Despite being weak, I managed to get off the bed unaided; little did I know that this would be one of the very last times that I would be able to do this and stand in front of the machine. Holding onto the handles, I stiffen my frame and hold my breath to ensure the image isn't blurry--anything to make the radiographer's night easier. The porter who has waited outside the closed doors for me takes me back to my cubicle on A&E; he wheels me in, locks all of the trolley wheels, pulls one of the sides down so I can exit the bed if I need to, wishes me well, and then off he goes to wheel the next patient to their destination.

I had hardly settled into my surroundings when a doctor pushed the curtain back,

'Bad news, Lisa, you have COVID. We will admit you for a few days to monitor you as a precaution. As you are probably aware, due to your chemotherapy, you have a suppressed immune system, so we need to make sure that you don't develop any serious complications. I've also prescribed a five-day course of antivirals, which should make you feel better in no time. We are just waiting for a bed to become available, and then we'll move you. Any questions?'
Honestly? I couldn't think of a single one.

A porter arrives shortly afterwards and takes me to the Helena ward; I have my own room with an ensuite wet room. It is in the older part of the hospital, so the ward looks run down and tired. I assume that as they are gradually building new wings, this part will eventually be knocked down and replaced with a brand-spanking new one. The Brownsword unit, which holds the physiotherapy department, was completed a few years ago, and they are currently working on The Dyson Centre, which, when completed, will be a state-of-the-art Cancer unit. According to the plans, the building looks fantastic, with lots of open space for the patients to sit in secluded solitude if they wish to.

The staff on the ward are great; they are very attentive when they take my observations and bring my meals, but they don't hang around to talk. I can't say that I blame them, but I am bored and lonely. Simon has also developed COVID-19, so he is unable to visit as he is really poorly at home; Harrison is looking after him. Rachael would usually have popped over to check on them and then visit me, but as she is pregnant, we can't take that risk.

The brain fog that the chemotherapy has caused won't allow me to concentrate on anything, so reading my book is out, and I even struggle to play the simplest of games on my phone, so I spend all day asleep. Which I suppose is a good thing because, hopefully, I will get better quicker. Which also means that I will be home quicker. People who know us would assume that because Simons's career took him away from home a lot, from the time Harrison was roughly seven months old, he would travel the globe with his job, and we would have been used to being separated. We are in its essence, but it doesn't mean to say that we accept or revel in being apart; it has always been a means to an end, earning a wage to support the family. Years ago, I was told, 'The only reason that you two are still together is that Simon is never bloody home.' Which as you can imagine I found incredibly rude, the fact that despite being together for (in 2024) twenty-six years and have never argued, obviously didn't factor into this little insight into someone else's thoughts on our relationship.

After three days, my temperature had started to regulate, the antivirals had kicked in, and they had started to work their magic on me. There was a quiet knock on my door before a medical professional entered, telling me that I was being discharged and asking if there was anyone who could collect me. I tell them that at the moment, no, my husband also has COVID-19, and my daughter is pregnant. So they arrange for one of their private ambulances to collect me and take me home. They warned me that it could be anything from thirty minutes to three hours as they are quite busy.

I phone Simon to let him know that I'll be home at some point today. I start packing my bits and bobs away, making sure that I remember everything (I usually manage to leave something behind, no matter where I am) and then settle in for the long haul of waiting for my ride to come. No sooner had I sat on the bed than there was a 'knock-knock' on my door, and a lovely man with a wheelchair entered. My ride is here and a lot quicker than any of us expected. I tell him that I can walk, but apparently, it is hospital policy when transporting patients who have been admitted that they are transported safely. In my case, this means the use of a wheelchair, so I sit down, and he buckles me in (I felt like a naughty toddler, and that unless I am buckled securely in place, would do their utmost to run away). He is very chatty as he wheels me through the hospital corridors, telling me that I'll need to wrap up as it's pretty wet and cold outside. It's typical November weather, really.

I am not sure what I was expecting when they said that I'd be going home in a private ambulance, but I was wheeled up the ramp at the back of what looked like a people carrier type thing. The wheelchair is strapped in place, and then what can only be described as a 'belt and braces' scenario is that I am also belted into the ambulance with the seat belt. I think I am pretty secure now, so there is no fear that I will run away!

Once we were on our way, I texted Simon to let him know that I had left the hospital and that I should be home soon. Knowing that he was still unwell and that he was no doubt in bed, I asked him to make sure that he was dressed. I had somehow managed to leave my keys at home, so he had to let me in.

The driver was quite chatty, to begin with, but I think he could tell that I was exhausted and that talking was really quite painful for my poor throat, So the conversation petered out. I also kept nodding off with the vibration of the wheels on the road and then jumping awake if we broke suddenly or if the car hit a pothole or a raised drain cover. Either that or, if I am honest with myself, it was probably the sound of my own snoring that had woken me.

Before I knew it, we had pulled up outside my home. The lights were on, and it looked quite welcoming. The driver took my bags to the door and rang the bell. Simon must have been tracking me because he answered the door almost instantly. Taking my bags off of the driver, he thanked him for bringing me home.

The seatbelt around me is unclipped, the wheelchair is detached from the ambulance, and the ramp is put in place before I am wheeled down it. He wheels me to the step of my front door, unclips the belt keeping me secured in the chair, and then Simon helps me into the house. I thank the driver for bringing me home so quickly.

Once inside, with the front door closed and locked, I begin to relax. I'm home, I'm with Simon, and I'm safe.

Simon makes a cup of tea, and we sit in the lounge in silence, just content to be with each other again. Once I have finished drinking it, I tell him that I have to go to bed as I am exhausted. I climb into my comfortable bed, the mattress absorbing my aching body, and I drift off into a peaceful slumber.

I spend the next few days in bed. I am unsure if it is because I am unable or unwilling to get up, but I feel so much better when I do surface. I am still suffering from the side effects of the chemotherapy, but the COVID-19 symptoms are gone.

Simon, however, continued to suffer for a short time afterwards. He said that he was jealous that I had had the antivirals and recovered quicker than him! However, we were both left with an annoying cough for a good few months afterwards, which made people take a wide berth if they heard us coughing, especially if we were in the oncology department! The fact that people parted like the Red Sea when one of us began coughing helped ensure that there was a safe distance around me.

ONCOLOGY PHONE CALL

23rd November 2022

Despite the anti-nausea medication, which was only prescribed for three days immediately following treatment, I suffered awful nausea twenty-four hours a day throughout my entire treatment. After mentioning this, I was told that they would change the medication slightly, which would hopefully give me some respite from this. They also recommend that I eat ginger, either in the shape of biscuits or a special ginger sweet that you can buy, as this has been known to be beneficial for nausea.

I mention the other side effects that have impacted my life: dry mouth, fatigue, loss of sense of smell and taste. Unfortunately, there isn't an easy remedy for fatigue, and they suggest that I listen to my body and rest if needed. For the dry mouth side effect, they recommend freezing fresh pineapple. I can't remember the philosophy as to why this would work, but we did try it, and it did help slightly. The loss of senses is a known side effect of treatment, and there is nothing that they can do except reassure me that once the treatment has finished, they will come back relatively quickly.

If you have ever been unlucky enough to have contracted COVID-19 and suffered the side effects of loss of taste and smell, you will know how awful it actually is. You will probably also understand how much of our enjoyment of food centres around these senses. You find yourself eating for texture rather than taste. Chocolate, despite not being the best thing to consume, and I hasten to add that it was eaten in minimal quantities, was the only thing that I found that wasn't totally abhorrent in texture. I think the worst texture for me was Weetabix; not only did it look like cardboard, but the texture could only be likened to sopping wet cardboard. I still struggle today to eat this without having flashbacks.

Once the oncologist had finished asking her routine questions and offering any snippets of advice to manage the side effects, she said that she would speak to me after my scan later in the week to discuss the impact the treatment was having on the tumour.

CYST REMOVAL

I have had a cyst on my back for several years; I hadn't done anything about it because it didn't really impact my life at all. But Simon persuaded me to have it removed; I think he was secretly worried that it may have been a cancerous tumour. Simon made the appointment, and I attended my local doctor's surgery for a minor op. I wanted Simon to come in with me and record it. I have a secret obsession with Dr Pimple Popper, but try as I might, I couldn't persuade him to do it for me!

The area felt slightly uncomfortable once the local anaesthetic wore off, but that is to be expected. Overall, the operation went according to plan. The doctor told me that it looked like a normal cyst, but it would be sent away for testing anyway. I never heard back, so I assumed that there was nothing to worry about.

The stitches were due to be taken out in a week's time, which would be after my second chemotherapy. The thought of attending the doctor's surgery after chemotherapy filled me with anxiety. All I could think was that I would have a weakened immune system and I would be waiting in a surgery surrounded by sick people. I kept myself busy by doing my diamond art in a feeble attempt to try to stop these thoughts from invading my everyday life. Some days were easier than others.

NARVA DAVIDSON

When Lisa asked to write a paragraph for her book I thought "Ya, that will be easy" little did I know.

I've known Lisa for many years, usual thing, our kids went to the same school. Our friendship has grown alongside our children. We have shared laughter, tears, boob hugs (both big boob club) hospital visits, too much gin and not enough cups of tea. Then came 'The big C'.

Oct 2022, I had just got in the car to leave for a break away with the hubby when Lisa rung me. "I need to talk to you, can you come round?" Never felt friend guilt like I did that day, I couldn't be there for her when she needed me. The following day after her consultation with the breast cancer unit she got the diagnosis and rung me in Rome. Time stood still as I listened to her telling me it was Cancer. I never felt disbelief like I did, but I did tell her that we would fight it as there was no "her" it was "we" and "we" would see this through to the end and I kept this word. We exchanged words and the call ended, and I cried. I was so angry; 55,000 women are diagnosed with breast cancer a year and why Lisa? I'll answer that question later.

I'll condense the following 12/18 months; it was a rollercoaster and not a fun one. The chemo knocked her for six, 10 rounds with Mike Tyson. It depleted her of all the energy; her mobility was robbed, her concentration, taste buds, her beautiful hair, her energy. Lisa as we knew her had left the building for that period, and we wrapped her up in love and care while her delicate body coped with the on sought of drugs.

This was hard as a friend to see her like this, I wanted to take this away from her, I was angry and left her mentally and emotional exhausted after some visits as I poured my positive vibes into her space. I couldn't hug her due to compromised infections and this was hard, so hard. I felt guilty for feeling angry, and didn't know where to direct this anger, so I did what I do best and went shopping. Every chemo session, I did her a package of goodies to look forward too. PJs/ fluffy socks/lip salves/shower gels/candle/M&S Percy pigs/ mints/mouth wash, anything I would have liked, she got (including the penis lolly from Barcelona, and chocolates for Bruges) . I would send cards through the door when I couldn't see her in the time straight after chemo. Out of sight but certainly not out of mind. During this time Lisa had serious emergency hospital visits for complications, honest to God she is a cat with nine lives, and she bounces back. I went in and visited her after one such complication, she wasn't great let's be honest she was at deaths door with heart issues, but we still laughed it out, seeing the funny side of the disgusting high calorie drinks she had to have. Lisa will never know (well she does now) how worried we all were about her.......

I told Lisa on her first chemo session "You know that heavy feeling on your shoulders? Well, that's me giving you a hug" I meant it and reminded her every session I was with her, sat on her shoulders. I needed her to know she wasn't alone; at no point did I ever want her feeling this was an individual fight, we are a team and always will be. I treated Lisa as I would want a friend to treat me. We laughed on many occasions, we cried, we sat in silence. Laughter was our biggest weapon when fighting this battle. We spoke about life, cancer and more life, the cancer was all consuming however, there is more to life than this battle.

During this shit show, we lost dear Dotty dog, the beloved family dog. Dotty meant so much to Lisa and when Dotty passed over the rainbow bridge I sat with Lisa at home, ensuring she wasn't alone. This was heart breaking and pain no one should go through, I wanted to take this pain away from her but felt so hopeless.

Lisa allowed me to see her at her lowest points, the parts of cancer you will never see or understand unless you have journeyed through it with your own loved ones. The 'Big Cs' impact is huge, some people come together, as we did and some people walk away, Their loss, not yours, Lisa. When Lisa's physical health deteriorated, her mental health became my priority. As her friend I needed to understand how I could support her, so I reached out to the Cancer Unit in Bath. I spoke to the Macmillan support team and explained the situation, asking how best I could support my friend. From that phone call they are now supporting her through this new chapter, how to live with the consequences of the treatment.

Lisa is a warrior, a survivor, she packed her punches and raised her middle finger to 'The big C'. Cancer picked the wrong woman, the wrong support network, because Lisa, my friend stood and fought, she survived. Her mobility is returning, catching up with my one speed of walking - slow!

Lisa asked me to write this to tell you how I supported a friend with cancer. I was unapologetically myself. I was my friend's friend, her agony aunt, her personnel shopper, spa buddy (hard job but I do my best) her confidant. I made sure I asked about her family and her partner as these can too often be forgotten. You must make sure that whilst you are supporting your warrior friend that you are also kind to yourself, I was angry, I had questions, I needed to vent, I had the unconditional support of my Husband, Chris. No one is alone in this journey. Reach out to charities/support groups etc for advice or guidance. Don't be afraid to seek this support

So to answer - why Lisa? I don't know the answer, I wish I did but you, The Big C, chose the wrong woman, she is strong, we held her up. Lisa abolished you, all whilst still being her true, loud, sweary self.

To my friend Lisa, do not change, and my lovely, I'll See You Next Tuesday. x

PERIPHERALLY INSERTED CENTRAL CATHETER (PICC) LINE

25th November 2022

I have three appointments today: an ultrasound to determine whether the invading BFB has changed, a telephone appointment to discuss the scan results and the treatment plan moving forward, and then one for the PICC line insertion.

Simon is by my side, holding my hand for the ultrasound. Both of us crossed everything (metaphorically speaking), hoping that the two courses of chemo had started to kill off the tumour.

It was a male sonographer this time, which I found surprising. Being a female and being treated for breast cancer, you already feel pretty vulnerable. So, being scanned by a male doctor didn't seem right.

But in true Lisa fashion, I pulled my big girl pants up, undressed behind the screen, walked to the bed, climbed on, and waited for him to start. One thing I was always thankful for was the fact that they always warmed the lubricant that they used. I remember when I was pregnant with both of my children, this was never done. Yes, it eventually warmed up, but the shock of having a cold gel squirted onto you is not great.

When the sonographer said there hadn't been a significant change in the BFB, it felt like my world had broken into tiny pieces for a second time. The overall density hadn't changed; it had only changed in size by 2mm. Personally, I took that as a win; 2mm is 2mm after all. He then tells me that he doesn't think the chemotherapy is working as well as should be expected and that oncology will decide what to do next. The horrible black cloud with the words 'I'm going to die' circled in my head again, like an unwelcome storm cloud that refuses to dissipate.

I leave the Breast Unit in a state of shock; I am upset and confused. This man has just driven the fear of God into me without any reasoning behind it. Of course, he has to tell me the results, but why say that the chemotherapy isn't working? I considered making a complaint, but I decided I just wanted to get to the end of my treatment; I didn't want to dwell on things I couldn't change.

I sat in the patient waiting area in the reception of the hospital. I think this is where people dump their relatives whilst they go off to collect prescriptions, pop to the loo, visit the little shop that is run by the volunteers of the 'Friends of the RUH', or to collect their car. There wasn't any room in the Atrium cafe, so we decided to sit there and wait for our next appointment. Simon had gone to buy us a coffee each when my phone began to ring. It was the oncology department ready to discuss the next steps. She said that looking at the scan results, we would continue with the treatment plan as it is and that she could see no reason to deviate. I mentioned what the sonographer had said, and whilst I was talking, I could feel the telltale lump in my throat and the tears that were welling in the corner of my eyes; I tried my damnedest to hold it together. I was conscious that there were a lot of people milling around, and I didn't want them to know my business. Most people, when you tell them that you have cancer, look at you with such sympathy; I didn't want this from my friends and family, let alone from complete strangers. She apologised on behalf of the sonographer for how he relayed the information and said that although it was only a slight change, it was still a change.

The relief I felt cannot be described, but Simon could see it when he returned with our coffees and a cake each; well, it would be rude not to, wouldn't it? I told him what the oncologist said: I should just ignore the negativity we had been subjected to. The treatment will continue as planned; a reduction is still a reduction.

After devouring our pre-lunch snack, we made our way to the radiography department, where a medical professional would insert a PICC line. My friend Amie works there, so I quickly chatted with her before the procedure was undertaken.
The nurse briefly explained the procedure, and there is a

detailed explanation with diagrams at the back of the book.

I signed the consent form and was led to a large room with a bed that looked like an operating table in the middle. I dumped my coat and bag in the corner of the room out of the way and climbed onto the bed.

Because of my sleeping position and to minimise discomfort, I decided to have the PICC line inserted in my right arm. A board was attached to the side of the bed, enabling my arm to be at a ninety-degree angle to my body. The doctor numbed the area of insertion with a local anaesthetic, so hopefully, I wouldn't feel anything.

I watched with interest as the nurses (they may have a professional title, but I am unsure of what it would be) moved around the room at ease, putting each piece of equipment required for the procedure onto a tray and then onto a trolley next to me. It was obviously a very well-practiced routine.

A nurse stood on my left side the entire time the procedure was being done, rubbing my arm and talking to me to take my mind off of what was happening. As with everything to do with my problematic crappy veins, the procedure took longer than anticipated. Apparently, the vein that they needed to use was 1cm deep; once they struck gold, they then needed to try to get the guide needle in, at an impossible angle, into my vein. Luckily, they managed it; otherwise, I can only assume that it would have needed to be placed in my chest, which is not something I would have been best pleased about.

After they had successfully inserted the guide, they measured the distance from insertion up my arm across my shoulder and then down to the rough location of my heart. Some tubing was cut to this measurement and then fed through the guide into my vein, terminating near my heart.

I sometimes think ignorance is bliss, so I didn't research what was involved in this procedure. I was somewhat surprised that it finished close to my heart. I hoped and prayed that they hadn't measured incorrectly so as not to damage the most important muscle in my body. But sometimes, you have to put blind faith in the medical profession, and as I am not a doctor, I have no medical qualifications. However, I am a dab hand at putting a plaster on!

Looking back, I wish I had asked more questions or at least researched it. It may have helped curtail the crippling anxiety that I now suffer from, albeit not as bad as when I was going through treatment, the remnants are still there, and sometimes, it impacts my life so intensely that it stops me from doing or accomplishing things that I would like to. There are only so many times that you can pull up your big girl pants without giving yourself a wedgie or a camel toe to rival all camel toes!

Once the procedure was complete, I hopped off the bed, grabbed my coat and bag, thanked the staff for looking after me and then made my way to the day patients area on the oncology ward.

I had to wait some time in the waiting room. My throat was parched from all the talking, and I now wished that I had swung past the cafe and grabbed a coffee to go. But never mind--I didn't have this foresight.

When my name was called, I followed the nurse and took the seat that was offered to me. The seats are the same as the ones in the Chemotherapy unit, but I resisted reclining the back and putting the footrest up, which I am quite pleased about because I was barely there for five minutes. A nurse handed me a carrier with some medical supplies: vials of saline, needles, gauze, bandages and one of those special buckets for sharps. There was also a leaflet for a special shower cover sleeve, which I would need to purchase as if the area were to get wet, it could lead to complications. She told me that she had made an appointment with the district nurse operating from my local doctor's surgery and that I would need to make an appointment to see her weekly.

The PICC line needs special care, or it can become infected. So every 7-10 days, you need to attend an appointment so that a medical professional can clean around the intravenous stopper (bung), flush the line through with a saline solution, put on a new bung, remove the dressing and clean the insertion area before placing a new dressing on and cutting some fresh tubing to cover the area to keep it as clean as possible.

As soon as this was all explained to me, I was free to leave the unit. I grabbed Simon from the waiting area, and we made our way to the car. Once we had left the hospital grounds, it was the usual round-robin of calls and messages. With almost immediate responses from most of the people on my round-robin contact list, I felt slightly overwhelmed by their kindness.

When I arrived home, the day's emotions left me feeling exhausted, so I went straight to bed. Trying to get comfortable with a tube sticking out of my arm was hard, but eventually, I found the perfect position.

Luckily, Simon was proactive as always and ordered a special waterproof arm cover, which meant I was free to shower without worrying about duck-taping my arm into a plastic bag.

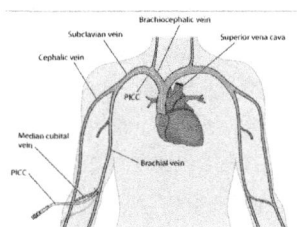

Diagram showing placement of PICC Line

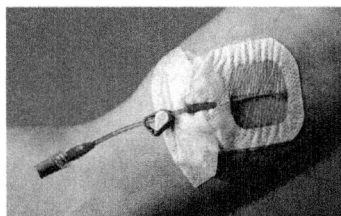

Picture of PICC Line in-situ

THIRD CHEMOTHERAPY TREATMENT

28th November 2022

Here we are, following the same routine, getting up super early as we need to be at the hospital at 9 a.m. for my treatment. I may have failed to mention that every infusion appointment was at 9 a.m. The hospital is only 15 miles away, but it doesn't matter which way you attack Bath; you can guarantee you will get held up in traffic. For this reason, we always aim to leave before 8 a.m.

The main route we usually would take is subject to flooding if there was anything more than a light shower. When this happened, the road would be closed. But unfortunately, the powers that be haven't had the foresight to install a sign or light system at the junction of this road, so you don't realise until you are right on it. Invariably, in the UK, we can get torrential downpours in the autumn/winter/spring/ summer, or any season. Luckily, there are several ways out of the town, so when this happens, we go a different route, the long way round through Shaw, but it minimised the risk of getting caught up in flood waters or losing time in having to turn around and join the convoy of cars doing the same thing.

When I arrived at the hospital, Simon dropped me off at the main entrance before parking the car. Despite leaving early, you can never tell when you will arrive. I walked through the already busy hospital towards the oncology department, checked in at reception, and headed to the chemotherapy unit. I checked in at the Chemotherapy Unit's reception and then went through the same procedure: removing my mask, washing and drying my hands, and putting a fresh mask on. They take their infection control seriously here.

I plonk myself on an available chair and take out my knitting (I haven't been able to knit for a good many years due to repetitive strain from sewing, but since stopping this, I can now knit again). Simon has placed his orders, and I am making him a pair of socks. The next project has already been chosen: a cardigan with a complicated cable pattern in a rust-coloured yarn. One day, I may actually be able to make something for myself!

As per the previous two times I have been here, my infusion is delayed, but with my boredom-busting bag at my side, I am not too bothered by this. I have plenty of activities to keep me occupied, as well as a blanket if I get cold or tired.

Most of the patients are kind and caring towards the staff. Unfortunately, there is always that one who believes they are entitled to better treatment than everyone else. I will never know how the staff manage to keep their cool when a patient is outright rude to them. It must be so stressful for them, and I would not wish their jobs on my worst enemy.

Once the infusion arrives, there is the usual flurry of activity, but this time, there is no need to cannulate me anymore, as everything is administered through the PICC line. While I didn't like looking at this foreign object jutting from my arm, I was thankful that I had had it done, as it meant that the treatment was easier and quicker, and the nurses were no longer feeling stressed about trying and failing to cannulate me.

The unit is a well-oiled machine, so there is no need to repeat the details of the infusion, but it went much the way of the previous two. How's my mental health doing? It's much the same as previously, but it gets slightly worse with each treatment.

I made the same round-robin of calls and texts on the way home, and once I had completed them, I fell asleep. I only woke up when we got home, and then I went straight to bed.

Top tip: find something that occupies your mind.

DOCTORS APPOINTMENT FOR PICC LINE MAINTENANCE

Doctors

My anxiety is through the roof. Today, I have to go to the doctor's surgery to have my PICC line flushed and the stitches on my back removed. The reason that I am so anxious is that I have to sit in the waiting room, no doubt surrounded by poorly sick people. But it needs to be done, so it is best to get on with it.

I am so weak I can barely stand unaided. Simon has to help me out of bed and onto the toilet, as well as help me sit and stand from the sofa. On a bad day, he has to hold both of my hands and walk backwards to keep me standing.

He parks as close to the surgery as possible and helps me inside; we had already decided that he would wait for me in the car to minimise the risk of infection. I felt a bit stronger today as I had spent the previous day in bed, trying to conserve as much energy as possible.

I hear my name being called. Looking up, I see a nurse standing by the open door leading to the corridor where the doctors' offices are. I walk slowly and shakily, trying to maintain a conversation with the nurse who is leading me to the nurse's room.

The district nurse, Tara, is absolutely lovely. She calms me down and says we'll do the flush first, then tackle the stitches. Taking my coat off and pulling my arm out of my jumper and t-shirt sleeve, I place my arm on the desk in front of her, ready for her to begin the cleaning procedure; again, I have included an online search, which goes into more detail below.

Once Tara had completed flushing and cleaning my PICC Line, I stood up and turned around so she could access my back; I almost immediately felt dizzy. I told the staff, and they quickly moved me to a chair before I collapsed. I asked them to carry on with removing the stitches and that I was okay. The dizziness got worse, so I was moved to lie on the bed, and one of the nurses went outside to find Simon; there was no way that I would have been able to make it back to the car unaided without being rendered unconscious.

Tara said she can visit me at home each week if it is easier. As I didn't want to inconvenience her, I told her I was more than happy to attend the surgery. But after she told me that some people should stay at home, with a community nurse visiting them, and that she believed that I fall into this category, I relented, and Tara made an appointment for the following week. She also arranged for a wheelchair to be delivered after I mentioned I am finding it difficult to leave the house and only do so for hospital or doctor's appointments.

There was a quick tap at the door, and the nurse reappeared with a worried-looking Simon. He helped me sit up and get dressed, paying particular attention to not touching the line, as it was still quite sensitive.

Tara informs him that there will be a wheelchair delivered and that in future, someone will visit me, so there is no need for me to attend the surgery any more.

With Simon on one side and a nurse on the other to keep me upright, we made slow progress back to the car. With the nurse ensuring that the seatbelt adequately restrained me, we said goodbye and thanks before heading home. Once home, I was delivered to the sofa, lying down with the TV on. I fell asleep in hardly any time at all. I woke sometime later, covered in one of our blankets, showing me that despite working, Simon would pop in and check on me throughout the day.

ONCOLOGY APPOINTMENT

14th December 2022

We are at the hospital again for another face-to-face appointment, this time it is to discuss the next three treatments, which will be different from the previous ones. The oncologist that we see is very young and very nervous.

She explains the side effects that the treatment can cause, including pins and needles and pain in your hands and feet. I tell her that I have already experienced these symptoms. I was somewhat surprised that she refused to accept that it had anything to do with the treatment that I had already received. The oncologist brushed my claims of already experiencing these symptoms under the carpet. I still maintain that if someone had listened to me on at least one of the multiple times I mentioned this, I would not still be suffering the debilitating effects that I continue to suffer with. However, this cannot be proven, as the condition I now have is so rare that no research (that I am aware of, and if any research has been done, it is a closely guarded secret) has been done.

The support medication that I need to take has also slightly changed; they are adding another anti-nausea drug, as well as increasing the dose of steroids that I need to take; instead of starting the steroids on the morning of the treatment, I now have to start them the morning before. I am glad that Simon is with me, as the brain fog is so bad I am sometimes lucky if I can string a sentence together without stumbling on my words or forgetting what I wanted to say entirely.

RACHEL HAYWARD

Rachel Hayward - I spoke to Rachel Hayward around this time. I tried to keep in touch with everyone through the chat page, but sometimes it was nice to have a conversation and hear someone's voice. We had a lovely little catch-up. She told me about the drama in her life, and I tried to offer advice. I'm not sure if she followed my advice, but it was nice to feel that I could still do this.

I mentioned that my mental health isn't great, which she said that it isn't surprising considering everything that I have gone through. Revealing that my mental health was suffering was difficult to do, although we are aware that a lot of people can struggle at some point in their lives, telling someone this I found difficult.

A few days later, a lovely little pink rose bush arrived in the post, with a little note from Rachel, saying that she wanted to send a bottle of gin, but as I am not allowed to drink, the rose would have to do. Her thoughtfulness brought a tear to my eye, and I immediately thanked her for the gift.

FOURTH CHEMOTHERAPY TREATMENT

19th December 2022

Here we are again for our next round of treatment. My blood pressure is through the roof, but considering everything I have been through, I am not surprised. The nurse orders an ECG as a precautionary measure. I have had so many of these performed on me since being diagnosed that I offer up my wrists and take my boots off so that they can attach the sensors more easily.

I watch the machine take the reading, which is then sent off for analysis before they can treat me.

They check that the PICC line is working by attaching a syringe and drawing blood before hooking up an IV drip into the line. This is to ensure that there aren't any problems when they begin the infusion.

There are the usual sounds associated with the unit: the nurses scurrying from one task to the other, some patients being less patient than they should be in their current situation, and the trill of beeps as the pumps come to the end of their allotted time.

The analysis has returned, and they have been given the all-clear to treat me. I was beginning to panic, as it seemed to take an awful long time for this to come back. All I could think was, 'What if they won't treat me? 'Will it affect the outcome?'

The nurse who was administering my infusion warned me that some of the side effects could be instantaneous, and she reeled them off; they sounded similar to anaphylactic shock. If it happened, they would stop the infusion, give me an injection and then start it again half an hour later.

Thankfully, I didn't appear to suffer from any of these side effects, but unfortunately, I did suffer from all of the others associated with Chemotherapy treatment.

Again, apart from this slight change, the treatment went as

expected. Once I had finished my treatment, I walked back to the waiting room, grabbed Simon, and went home, obviously making the usual round-robin of calls and texts during our journey.

CHRISTMAS DAY AND THIRD HOSPITAL ADMISSION

25th December 2022 - It's Christmas Day!
Simon and I would typically have a breakfast of smoked salmon and scrambled eggs; Harrison, not being a lover of smoked salmon, would have either scrambled eggs or cereal. We would then start the veg prep together, put the roast in the oven, pour a glass of something nice, and wait for Rachael and Jamie to come over for the afternoon.

This year was very different; my breakfast consisted of a handful of pills, followed by being stabbed in the stomach by Simon.

Rachael and Jamie arrived early and started making the Christmas lunch. They brought everything with them, and Jamie has even made his amazing roast potatoes. I don't know what he does to them, but they are some of the best that I have ever had. They set to work in the kitchen, and I can hear Simon offering his assistance. He is obviously trying to help, although they probably think that he is interfering.

With Simon's assistance, I slowly made my way downstairs. I wanted to pop into the kitchen, which would have only been ten more steps, but I didn't have the energy. I took up my usual perch on the sofa and did the daily routine of putting the TV on and then promptly falling asleep.

Simon woke me later to take more medication; he told me that lunch was also ready. With Simon walking backwards, holding both of my hands to keep me upright, I made very slow progress to the kitchen, stopping occasionally when my legs threatened to give way.

I wish I could tell you that the food Rachael and Jamie had prepared smelled lovely, but unfortunately, I can't. Not because it didn't--I am almost positive that it did--but along with my sense of taste, I had also lost my sense of smell. So you basically ate on texture alone. The joy of eating had all but been taken from me.

Rachael put a small amount of each offering on my plate. I took a few mouthfuls and couldn't manage anymore. I felt awful. Everything hurt, including my eyes. I just wanted to sleep.

The kids had worked so hard to make this Christmas as normal as possible, and I felt I had ruined it for them. Due to finances, the presents were meagre, a box of chocolates and some socks each. Looking at the gifts underneath the tree the night before really upset me; we would generally be able to buy the kids a few nice presents, and they always had a stocking filled with gifts. Simon and I would generally club together and buy a joint present or get each other a token present. We would use the money we had saved and go for a nice meal later. We would also typically buy a token present for a few close friends. This year, there were only half a dozen presents underneath the tree, and it made me feel like a failure.

Despite being exhausted, I wanted to stay up and play board games or watch a film, which was a family tradition after we'd eaten lunch and tidied up.

Do you remember the year that 'Pie-face' was all the rage? We only played it for one year, as after someone tried to cheat, it turned into a full-on food fight; we raided the fridge for anything we could throw at each other, and then came the jugs of water. Poor Jamie stood in the corner of the kitchen, as far away from us mentally challenged ones as humanly possible. When we had finally finished, either through needing to catch our breaths from laughing so much or because we had run out of things to throw, he looked utterly shocked and said, 'You lot are nuts!'

When I think back, every game we played ended in unruliness. Even 'Pinch or Pass,' which is quite a sedate game, really, ended up with us chasing each other around the lounge, trying to grab each other's cards.

Nerf wars have always been a particular favourite for our mental family. You have to feel a little bit sorry for our neighbours.

We don't do quiet; we are all loud and boisterous.

I apologised to everyone and told them I wanted to go to bed. Simon and Jamie helped me climb the stairs, which felt as if I were scaling Mount Everest. With one of them behind, pushing me, and the other in front pulling me, we managed to make it to the top of the mountain without crumbling into a heap.

Simon helped me undress; when I was sitting on the edge of the bed, he lifted my legs and swung me around gradually so I was lying down. I cannot explain or put into words the excruciating pain that I was actually in following my fourth treatment. If you can, try to imagine the worst bone pain you have ever experienced, then times it by at least 100. My entire skeleton hurt; it felt as if every single bone was being simultaneously attacked by sledgehammers over and over again. If I had been able to throw myself off a cliff, safe in the knowledge that this would have brought me some relief, then I would have. Even the slightest of movements would cause a ricochet of pain through my entire body.

The sounds of my family in the kitchen below me, laughing and joking, enjoying the remainder of Christmas Day, travelled through the floor. I could hear them becoming louder as the alcohol hit their systems. I begin to cry, feeling like an alien in my home, wanting so badly to take part in the festivities, but unable to. It felt as if my heart was breaking. I gradually drifted off to sleep, praying that during my slumber, I would have some relief from the pain.

My sleep was disturbed sometime later when a slightly tipsy Simon came to bed. All of a sudden, I was busting to use the toilet, so Simon helped me out of bed and into the bathroom.

'How are you feeling?'

'Like shit, everything hurts, even my eyes.'

Before I knew it, he had grabbed the thermometer and stuck it in my ear while I was sitting on the toilet, minding my own business. It shrills a warning that my temperature is high, 40.1 degrees to be exact. He shows me the readout and says that he'll phone the emergency line.

'I am not going to hospital on Christmas Day!'

He retakes my temperature, shows me the readout, and gives me his 'really' face, raising his eyebrows as far as they would go.

'Fine, call them,' I said, trying my hardest to maintain adult composure when what I really wanted to do was throw my rattle out of the pram and stamp my feet.

Listening to the one-sided phone conversation, I succumbed to my fate, knowing that I would be going to the hospital. Luckily, due to her pregnancy, Rachael hadn't been drinking. Simon wasn't drunk, but he was probably over the legal limit, so we had to wake Rachael to drive us in.

I don't know how they did it, as I was so weak, but with Jamie's help, they managed to get me downstairs and into Rachael's car. I don't remember the drive there, so I must have fallen asleep immediately.

I do not remember much about this admission. Much of the information comes to me in flashbacks when I least expect it. After speaking with Simon, Rachael, and a few others, I realise they have filled in some of the gaps for me.

After buzzing the bell to the Medical Assessment Unit (MAU), I was admitted to the ward and given a side room. The nurse on the unit took my observations and blood. My temperature had continued to rise during the drive over, so antibiotics were connected to my PICC line within twenty minutes of arriving at the hospital, which was unusually quick.

Rachael and Simon stayed with me for a few hours, although I wasn't aware of their presence or the presence of the medical staff, who would frequently come into the room to check on my progress. An ECG was performed as my heart rate was quite high.

I was unable to move unaided; Simon would have to help me use the toilet, holding onto me so I wouldn't fall off. When Simon eventually had to leave, the nursing staff would perform this service.

At some point, a bed became available in the William Budd ward, which is the ward that specialises in treating cancer patients; a porter arrived and moved me along with my possessions to the waiting bed. I did not want to be on this ward. In my head, I thought that I would find myself surrounded by cancer patients in various stages of dying. It couldn't have been further from the truth. Because of their suppressed immunity, each patient has their own room. The bathroom facilities have to be shared, but as I was so weak and poorly, a nurse wheeled a commode into my room for me to use until I was strong enough to walk across the hall to use the facilities.

My room was a good size, with a sink and mirror so you could wash and brush your teeth if you felt strong enough. I also had air conditioning and a small TV attached to the wall behind the bed, which you could move towards you. I couldn't look at the ill-fitting curtains. Still, I considered putting a picture on the 'CABMFF' page, a Facebook page for curtain, soft furnishing makers, interior designers or anyone in the trade. They are a lovely bunch, and a few of them sent me cards and flowers when I broke the news of my diagnosis. We all advise on different methods and where to find certain fabrics. But I decided against posting it, mainly due to the sympathetic responses that I would no doubt receive.

Despite having my boredom-busting bag, Simon paid for a twenty-four-hour pass on the TV. Most of the time, I would have the TV on as a way of breaking up the silence when I was on my own, but I wasn't really watching it. When Simon came in, we would watch a film together, with him pulling the chair as close to me and the bed as possible, and we would always hold hands while we watched it.

The nurses came in frequently to check on me, do my observations, and swap the saline drip for more antibiotics.

After a couple of days, two oncology team members visited me, one with a laptop, taking notes while the other spoke to me. Seeing Simon sitting in my room outside of visiting hours, she asked if I knew him. I thought that this was a particularly strange thing to ask, so I replied, 'No, it's just some random that I picked up from the street.' Note to self: Some oncologists do not have a sense of humour.

'So you don't know him then?' Confusion is showing on her face.

'He's my husband; of course, I know him!' I am now much more cautious of what I say, as some people can't crack a smile, and I swear she was about to call security to remove Simon.

I can't remember what the oncologist said, and much of what she said didn't make it through my ear canal to my brain, so I was pleased that Simon was there to act on my behalf. But the upshot was that I am responding well to the antibiotics, and as soon as my temperature remains stable, with no spikes, for at least twenty-four hours, I can go home. From this point on, every time my temperature was taken, I would ask what it was, praying that it hadn't spiked.

Eventually, my temperature stabilised, and the medical professionals deemed me well enough to be discharged with a five-day course of oral antibiotics.

As soon as I got home, Rachael video-called me. I hadn't seen her since Christmas Day, so we made plans for her to come over and take me for a drive-through coffee. Despite feeling extremely weak, I really enjoyed these little outings with her. It was the only time I left the house without it involving going to the doctor's surgery or a hospital appointment or admission.

I always thought that there was a golden rule of what not to say to a cancer patient, 'do you think you're going to make it?' being the main one. So when these words were uttered to me by a new district nurse when he came to clean and dress my PICC line, I was flabbergasted!

'Of course, I F******G am!' That was the only response I could think of. After he left, I couldn't help but let the dark thoughts enter my head again. I found myself believing that they knew something that I didn't and that it was written somewhere on my notes that they didn't expect me to survive this.

After a couple of days of thinking about it, I decided to report it to his supervisors. I did this not to cause him any trouble but to ensure that he gets some more training on what is and isn't acceptable. The team assured us that he wouldn't be visiting me again.

Simon has been extremely busy up to this point; not only has he been working full time, but he has also been taking care of me, keeping the housework up together, spending time with Harrison, as well as moving his office, which was on the second floor, into our snug opposite the lounge. The snug started out as our dining room, but it eventually became a dumping ground, and then a snug, and then I started using it as a store room. I would store all of my fabric sample books and finished jobs on some shelves that I had purchased.

In an effort to clear the room, we sold off the fabric sample books and hangers, the leftover rolls of linings, and anything else that we could, bit by bit. The corner sofa was dismantled and put in the 'Harry Potter' cupboard at the top of the house.

Eventually, Simon managed to move his office to the ground floor, which meant he could keep a better eye on me. We bought a bed and turned his old office into a spare room in case any

Lisa Jane Holman

family members decided to come and stay.

As my dad would threaten to visit us and stay overnight, Simon said that he wanted to make the room comfortable for him and that he had decided to buy an electric blanket. While he was on the phone with John Lewis in Cribbs Causeway to check if they had what he wanted in stock, I looked on the Mall website to see what accessibility they have. I was so excited when I saw that they loan electric wheelchairs and mobility scooters to shoppers for free. As soon as he is off the phone, I tell him that I'm coming with him and that he needs to phone up and book a wheelchair for me.

It was so nice to be able to do 'normal' things together again. We went for lunch and looked around the shops. After our little excursion, I was so tired that I slept all the way home, but I felt overjoyed that we had found this.

Visiting Cribbs Causeway became a regular occurrence, mostly just to get out of the house. We would have lunch, look around the shops, bulk at the price of some of the items, and then go home.

On one of these trips, Simon came to the car with a mobility scooter instead of an electric wheelchair. To begin with, I didn't want to get on it; I had always associated this kind of aid with older people, but I am glad that I listened to him and tried it. He was right; it was much easier to steer than the wheelchairs. However, I would still underestimate corners and end up mounting some of the displays or dragging them along until I realised. It should honestly be a comedy sketch.

FAIRWELL MY FAITHFUL FRIEND

5th January 2023

When my sister passed, she left behind a menagerie of animals. There was Vander, her horse, a cat called Soggy, and then three dogs; she originally had four but had re-homed Harley, a hunter-way cross, a few months before she left us. Max was a black-and-white mongrel, Ella was a sausage dog, and Dottie was a show cocker spaniel puppy.

Vander stayed where he was; luckily, he already lived on my dad and Sue's property, so they took care of him and Soggy.

Max went to Faye's partner Dave, Mum had Ella, and I inherited Dottie.

Dottie was the most mental dog I had ever known; she was more duck than dog; if she even caught wind of the slightest amount of water, she would dive straight into it, not caring if it was more mud than water.

The day before my diagnosis, we had to have our King Charles Spaniel, Charlie, put to sleep. He was getting on in years and hadn't had the best start in life; we were his fifth owners, and when we re-homed him, he was just five years old. For this reason, he had many problems and was extremely stubborn. Watching him slowly drift off to sleep, knowing that we would be leaving the vets with just his harness and lead, was horrendous. Charlie was always more Simons dog than mine, this is because Dottie had firmly claimed me as her owner, and as far as she was concerned, Charlie wasn't allowed near me.

Dottie hadn't been herself for a few days, nothing that we could put our finger on; she was eating and drinking, but she had become incredibly quiet; she didn't zoom around anymore. Simon had to take her to the Vet without me, as we were expecting the district nurse to visit to do my PICC line and to take blood in readiness for my fifth round of Chemotherapy. Tara arrived just as Simon was about to leave; she loved Dottie and always made a fuss of her. Having a spaniel at home herself, she loved all spaniels. Tara was still with me when Simon phoned with the awful news that Dottie had heart failure. The Vet told Simon that we could give her medication to help, but that, in turn, could lead to multiple organ failures; while I wanted to keep my fur baby with me, I knew that it wouldn't be fair and to do so would be incredibly selfish. I told Simon I didn't want to go down that route, and he responded that he knew what he had to do. Through my tears, I told him that he had to bring her home first so that I could say goodbye.

I was inconsolable. Tara held me until I managed to pull myself together and stop crying. She stayed with me until Simon returned to make sure that I wasn't on my own after hearing this upsetting news.

As Dottie was Faye's last living pet and our last connection to her, I told the rest of the family what had happened and what we had decided to do. Everyone was extremely upset, as I am sure you can imagine. For me, it felt as if I was losing Faye all over again.

We decided that Simon would take her back the following day, and I spent the night on the sofa with her, ensuring she felt loved.

Harrison went with Simon to the vets the following day, one for moral support and two so that he could say goodbye. I wasn't able to go because my immune system is so weak that if someone were to sneeze in the next town, I would get a cold.

I sat in silence, with Narva holding me, watching the time on my phone tick down to the appointment time, knowing that Dottie and Faye would be reunited within five or ten minutes. The tears silently flowed from my eyes and pooled in my lap. I made no attempt to brush them aside, giving myself these few minutes to sink into my grief.

When Simon and Harrison returned, they silently put away Dottie's harness and lead and began moving her bed from underneath the stairs so that there wouldn't be a constant reminder that she was missing when I walked past.

KARIN BEASANT

For Lisa,

Cancer, a word that instils fear and dread, not just for the poor soul who has a fight of their life, but also to the family and friends who face an unknown enemy, with no idea of what to do or say that can help a family member or friend.

I first met Lisa many years ago at a paranormal event and we became para friends.

It was when she joined the Jamaica Inn Paranormal team that our friendship grew into a close bond and understanding with each other. She is extremely gifted in so many ways, creative, funny and the mind of a smart businesswoman.

I am honoured to be her friend, but know my own faults well, how she puts up with me, I have no idea, but tolerance springs to mind mostly.

I will never forget the first sign, when she mentioned that she felt a lump in her breast, I thought it would be nothing, but as my cousin had recently survived her breast cancer, thought it would be an easy fix. How wrong I was.

When she told me that not only she had breast cancer, but stage four, a life threatening fight of her life, I was so scared, not just for her, but how me, a person who doesn't do hugs and affection could support her.

The first instinct is to run away, hide from the situation, pretend it doesn't exist, but I knew that I had to kick myself up the backside and be there, not matter how uncomfortable it would make me, as my feelings would not matter, I didn't want to lose another friend, this time I would do what I can in my way.

When Lisa told me not to treat her differently, use our unconventional humour to call her cancer Mr Bean, it was music to my ears and the greatest sense of relief for me, very selfish I know, but here was something I could do, help in my way, by being an utter twat, idiot, clown to when she needed to forget her distress, her pain and dread of the future.

No one wants to think of death, leaving a husband, son, family and friends behind, so I put my big girl pants on, (I don't wear any) and became her personal joker.

The phone calls, visits, seeing this wonderful lady go through such awful treatment to save her life, I took the utter piss out of her.

Shocking isn't it, but boy it felt good, because we were telling that cancer it would not live, it would die because she will fight with every ounce of her strength.

Boy did I lie about how awful she looked. I lied to her about her hospital do not resuscitate form, I lied about the future, as I wanted selfishly to not lose her.

She is my friend.

When she became better and I could take her on our paranormal nights, I had to learn to undress her, help her with cutting of her food, (I did struggle, but humour makes the medicine go down easier.

We cried with laughter trying to get her up stairs of hotels, trying to get her arse out of her clothing, was akin to dressing a dead fish, as she couldn't move, but laugh we did.

Her fake boob in her bra, boy that weighed a ton, I dread to think what mine weigh, but to put her fake boob in her bra on my head and ask if I look a right tit, is the Monty Python humour I grew up with.

Taking Lisa speeding in her chair, pretending to let go was some of my best memories to date.

Even when my cousin rang me to say she had breast cancer a few years ago, I replied how can she as she has not tits, this is me, a wally but humour can fit anything life throws at you.

Don't be afraid to say silly things, laughter is the best medicine for illness, don't run away, tempting though it is, I nearly did and would have regretted it for the rest of my life.

Don't put off doing the things you talk about with friends and family, do it now, as no one knows what the future holds for any of us.

Be there, care, but poke fun, make wonderful memories.

Bloody crying writing this, so Lisa, bugger off now, I need a cup of tea.

Karin

FIFTH CHEMOTHERAPY TREATMENT

9th Jan 2023

Round five of Chemotherapy went the same as the others. My blood pressure is still through the roof, so another ECG is ordered. It comes back fine, so the treatment continues.

I busy myself knitting or reading my book, waiting for the infusion to arrive. It finally does, and then, as with the previous times, the prescribed infusion is checked as being correct, my identity is double-checked, and off we go--the infusion begins.

Once it is completed, I leave the unit. I find Simon in the corner of the waiting room, busy beavering away with work. He sees me approaching, packs up his bits' n' bobs, and we make our way to the car. Then, it is the usual round-robin of calls and texts. Once we are home, I go to bed, falling asleep straight away due to sheer exhaustion.

FOURTH HOSPITAL ADMISSION

14th Jan 2023

Apparently, although I don't remember this, Narva visited me with one of her chemo care packages. I couldn't read the words on the box she gave me, as I struggled to focus on anything. She went into the kitchen and told Simon that she was concerned about me, that I was not very well at all, and that she felt that I should be in Hospital.

Simon reassured her that this is how I usually am at this stage after Chemotherapy, which is true; however, we didn't realise how quickly I would go downhill.

After she left, it wasn't long before we had to call the 24-hour helpline.

I can't believe it has happened again, another severe infection, another admittance to the Hospital. After being triaged on A&E, I was admitted to the cardiac ward; I suspect that this is because my resting heart rate is 168 bpm. It never even got that high after running for five miles. I asked the nurse why I was admitted to Cardiology, not the William Budd ward or another ward. He looked stunned, as if he were a rabbit caught in the headlights, and told me that as my immune system is compromised, it is the only place with a free bed. I didn't believe him but was too weak to challenge it.

The porters arrived, bickering over who was pushing and who would hold the doors open. It made me chuckle, so I waited for the younger lady to stamp her feet until she got her way. Her powers of reasoning were quite good, but they were nothing compared to the experience of the gentleman who won the argument. She bowed down and trotted in front, opening the doors and steering the front end of the trolley around the sharper corners.

When I arrived at the cardiac ward, there was a flurry of activity as the nurses settled me into bed. They made sure that I had everything that I needed before leaving. A nurse soon returned with the observation machine, which takes, stores, and uploads all of your readings. My heart rate and temperature are still high, and my blood pressure isn't tremendous, either.

Simon pays for the TV subscription again for me before leaving. I cry as he leaves, as I want him to stay, but I know that he has to go, as we still have Harrison to consider, who has been spending an inordinate amount of time alone.

The following day, Simon arrives just after breakfast with his laptop. Once breakfast is out of the way, the nurses change your bedding and make sure that you have managed to wash to freshen up, and then the doctors start their rounds. The cardiologist visits us, telling us that I am extremely poorly and what the plan of action is. They will do a more detailed ECG*; if it shows that my heart rate, although high, is beating a regular rhythm, then they won't intervene. If it doesn't, then we will discuss the next steps. Simon asks how long they expect me to be in the Hospital; the cardiologist says definitely a few days, possibly a week or more.

When you are sick, it is strange how the mind plays tricks on you. You don't realise how poorly you actually are until you have come out of the other side and look back on what has happened.

Each time Simon came to visit, there would be a look of relief on his face that I was still there.

It is only recently that I have come to realise just how truly blessed I am to still be alive.

On one of the days that Simon had decided to pop into Bath town centre to pick up a few bits, a student doctor came to speak with me to get more information before the primary doctor did his rounds. She asked the standard questions and then made to leave the room before turning around and crouching by the bed next to me. The following conversation made me realise how poorly I was.

'Have you given any thought to signing a DNR*?'

'Er, no, why would I want to do that? I'll be going home soon.'

'When a patient's heart works as hard as yours, we ask them to think about this.' 'Regardless, I would want to be resuscitated*.'

'Do you know what is involved in resuscitation?' She then proceeds to tell me exactly what it means to be resuscitated, along with the implications of broken ribs, bruising and difficulty with breathing.

'But I'd still be alive.'

After the doctor left, I phoned Karin in tears, absolutely hysterical, telling her that they wanted me to sign a DNR. I don't know how she did it, but she calmed me down and managed to persuade me that it was common practice; despite me telling her that they hadn't done it previously, she convinced me that they had probably forgotten. Unbeknownst to me, she then phoned Simon and told him what had happened and that they had to lie to me, or I might just give up.

It wasn't until I caught a news report on DNR orders sometime in 2023 that I realised they had lied to me. The reporter informed the viewers that a Hospital would only ask you to sign a DNR if they do not expect you to recover. If I had known this then, I would have given up. Because, after all, if the professionals do not expect you to recover, what is the point in fighting? I will be forever thankful to both Simon and Karin, especially since I know how hard it was for them to keep such an enormous secret from me and how they both hate lying.

My PICC line had always been painful when it was being

cleaned and flushed. The slightest movement of it would create painful spasms up my arm, but after the last one, it had become excruciating, to the point that even moving my arm could illicit these painful spasms. I mentioned it to one of the nurses when she came in to change one of the drips over, as even this caused a tiny element of pain.

A short while later, one of the ladies who worked in the unit that inserts the PICC lines visited me. She confirmed there didn't appear to be an infection and asked how long it had been painful. I told her that it had always been slightly painful and would like to remind me that it was still there if I turned over in my sleep and applied slightly more pressure than usual. If I had known that this wasn't normal, I would have made sure I had that the nurse or doctor would have referred me to someone who would sort it out.

After examining the site closer, she determined that the metal clip that sits under the skin and keeps the PICC line in place touches a nerve, which is why I have always had problems with it.

She gave me two choices: I could leave it as it is, as I only have one round of treatment left, or she could attempt to remove the clip but keep the line in place. She warned me that, as it is touching a nerve, this could potentially be incredibly painful.

'So ouchy now? Then no ouchy later?' It was the only way I could formulate the question in my head.

She made me chuckle by repeating my exact words. I then elected to have the clip removed.

Along with the doctor who was going to do the procedure, two nurses were in my room. The doctor gave them instructions to hold me as still as possible, as she didn't want to risk the PICC line coming out completely. All I can say is that it bloody hurt, and I was glad when it was over. My eyes were leaking uncontrollably; one of the nurses showed me compassion by rubbing my legs once the procedure was over, telling me how great I had been and that it was all over now.

The doctor instructed the ward staff to check the port's situation each time they saw me to make sure that it hadn't moved. Although the dressing had a strong adhesive, so the port was pretty well stuck down, there is still the fear that it may start to come out of its own accord.

The relief from removing the clip was terrific; my arm no longer felt like a foreign object, and no pain was associated with moving or using it. It felt normal again.

Eventually, the antibiotics began to work, and my condition stabilised, so I was discharged with the usual five-day course of oral antibiotics. Being home, in my own bed, with my own things around me, I felt safe. There was no longer the fear of picking something up from visitors to my room. I told Simon to lock the doors, and I didn't want to see anyone until after the danger point of my last treatment had passed. Some may think this may have been overkill, but I didn't care; I didn't want a repeat visit to the Hospital.

ONCOLOGY APPOINTMENT

25th January 2023

This appointment was the only time I had seen an oncologist who asked if the wheelchair was normal for me. I honestly think that this woman saved my life.

On entering her office, she asked how I felt after my admission to the Hospital.

I told her that, honestly, I felt like death. I cannot even perform the simplest of tasks unaided. Even though he has a full-time job, Simon has become my full-time carer, which puts a lot of pressure on him.

Initially, she suggested that we reduce the dose of the Chemotherapy but halted; looking at me, she took in every detail about me. She asked if I usually had to use a wheelchair. After telling her that it wasn't and that before I began treatment, I was training for the Bath Half Marathon.

She took some time to review my medical notes on the computer screen, assessing the number of Hospitalisations I had had.

Then she told me the plan: we would reduce the dose, and I would have an extra week to recover before my final treatment.

I can't say that I was particularly happy about this plan; I couldn't help the dark thoughts that would creep into my head: '...will it still be as effective?' '...will the cancer spread further by reducing the dose' '...am I going to die?'

SURGICAL APPOINTMENT

25th January 2023
Our second appointment of the day was with my surgeon.

I had to attend an appointment for another ultrasound scan to see how much the tumour had shrunk before seeing her. As there seems to be with most situations, there was good and bad news. The bad news was that the overall size of the tumour hadn't changed. The good news was that it was less dense and had started to break apart into smaller pieces. More good news was that the cancer in my lymph nodes had also changed, being less dense and slightly smaller.

Waiting to see my surgeon, I was on tenterhooks, and I'm not sure why, to be honest. She has always been very kind and considerate each time we have seen her. But I suppose that because the tumour hasn't shrunk, I'm nervous about my options and whether she will say that it might be worth having more Chemotherapy treatment. A choice that I do not want to have to consider.

My surgeon assures me that although the overall size of the tumour hasn't shrunk, the fact that it is less dense and has begun to break apart is good news, so she schedules an appointment for my surgery, which would take place approximately six weeks after my last chemotherapy session.

My surgeon presents me with two options: I can have a lumpectomy or a mammoplasty. The lumpectomy is the less invasive option but doesn't always give the same results as the more invasive mammoplasty. As I want to give myself the best possible chance to be here for the long haul, I opt for the more invasive option. She confirms this is the right course of action for me, which I wish they would freely disclose at the outset of diagnosis.

She begins to check her diary, and I tell her due to the severity of the side effects that I have suffered, the oncology department has elected to postpone my last treatment by one week.

Her surprise when I reeled off everything that I had endured to date proves that there need to be more inter-department discussions when a patient is being seen by more than one department.

She asked if I wanted to continue with the chemotherapy treatment, and up to this point, I wasn't aware that I was entitled to decide not to continue. The option that I could elect to stop treatment had never been discussed with me by any department or medical professional that I had come into contact with on my numerous admissions. So, being told this now was a bit like shutting the gate after the horse had bolted. I told her that considering I had come this far and that I only had one treatment left, I might as well get it over and done with and that if she felt that the last treatment would have a positive overall effect on my prognosis, then I'll continue with the plan. She confirms that it would be beneficial to continue with the last treatment, so despite wanting to tell her that I'd rather not, I tell her that in that case, that is what we will do.

I have been given a provisional appointment for my surgery on 14th March. She informed me that I would receive an appointment letter in the post for my operation and my pre-op checkup.

Once we had discussed everything, we left with one of the Breast Care Nurses, who we followed to another room. She explained that as I will have a T-junction, the risk of infection or the wound breaking down is higher. For this reason, I would have a special bandage fitted to the surgical site called a portable negative pressure wound dressing*. The dressing is connected via a wire to a battery pack, which now and then increases the pressure on the wound, aiding blood flow to the area and helping with the healing process.

I would also have a drainage tube protruding from my armpit

area, which is connected to a bag to collect fluids. I am given a fabric bag, which looks similar to a shopping bag, to hold the battery pump for the dressing and the drainage bag. I am also given a heart shaped cushion to help keep me as comfortable as possible after the operation.

I always donated fabric scraps to Sally and her quilting group through my sewing business. They would use these scraps to make the bags and cushions for cancer patients, which they would donate to the RUH. In all the years I have donated to the group, I never once thought that one day, I would be receiving one of these. I didn't recognise any of the fabrics from which the gifted items were made. It is heartwarming to realise that it isn't just Sally's group that makes these for the Hospital. They have also made small quilts for premature babies in incubators and regularly donate funds or quilts to local charities.

The breast care nurse explains how to change the drain if it becomes full, and what to do if the pump stops working. She also informs us of any factors that we need to watch out for immediately following the surgery, which could point to a possible infection or the wound may have begun to break down.

Leaving the Hospital, I was silent, unable to speak while trying to quell the rising panic in my gut. Simon must have realised that I was fighting an internal battle, as he didn't try to engage me in conversation. I know that it is important that we are told of the worst-case scenario and given all of the facts, but I have always tried to maintain a positive mental attitude, and it just felt a bit like scaremongering.

I'm not saying that they should sugarcoat things, and I realise how important it is to ensure that patients are aware of every eventuality. I just wish that there could be some positivity as well.

SIXTH CHEMOTHERAPY TREATMENT

6th Feb 2023
I'm here! I finally made it to the end!!

The week before this treatment, I can actually say that I have felt more like myself than I have in a long time. I have had more energy, and I have been able to eat more. Yes, I still spend a lot of time asleep, but I have found that I have had the energy to do more of my diamond art, and Simon and I have even managed to take a few trips out in the car.

And the best thing of all? Today is the day that I have my PICC line removed! I simply cannot wait for this to happen. I have felt like I have been on the set of Star Trek, waiting for the Borg to finish assimilating me. I hated every second of having the PICC line, and I found the very sight of it repulsive.

I gifted the nurses in the chemotherapy unit chocolates and biscuits as a thank-you for looking after me during my treatment. Some of the patients are just downright rude and full of their whimsical belief in their own self-importance, so the nurses on the unit really do have a thankless task with some of their patients.

Once my infusion had been completed, I eagerly waited for the PICC line to be removed. A nurse told me that we had to wait until the oncology department confirmed that it was no longer required. I mentally crossed everything possible, and we were soon given the nod to remove it. Luckily, this worked, as one of the nurses came over to my chair with a tray of paraphernalia ready to remove it.

This is it. It's finally coming out!

But in true Lisa fashion, nothing is ever easy. The nurse can't get it out; for some reason, it is stuck. The nurse advised me to go home and come back in tomorrow, and they said they would try again.

I am pleased that it is being removed, but I wish I didn't have to come back for it to be done. I just want it all to be over.

When I returned the following day, the same nurse was able to remove it this time. Sometimes, this can happen, where the body swells at the site of trauma, and considering everything that I have been through, my whole body is one big pile of trauma.

FIFTH HOSPITAL ADMISSION

9th February 2023

It would appear that my body has more spanners to throw in the works; this time, my body has decided that I need to have a blood clot before surgery. Because you know, why the hell not?

So I am back in hospital, more scans and prodding and poking, along with another chest X-ray for good measure.

I have a 5cm clot that, as luck would have it, isn't in a central vein, although it is close to one. The doctor gives me two options again.

The first is to see how it goes. Sometimes, these things sort themselves out. They would monitor me regularly to see how it progresses. Option two is to take a course of blood thinners. I would need to be careful not to injure myself and carry a card around with me informing medical professionals that I was taking them. This course would finish a week before my surgery, so the natural clotting ability of my blood would have recovered in time.

Although the choice was mine, the doctor recommended option one, which could mean that the clot could get more extensive and then would delay my surgery. I ignored her and chose option two, which my surgeon confirmed was the right decision when speaking with her later.

AN UNEXPECTED VISIT

Between my final chemotherapy treatment and my surgery, I had an unexpected visit from a friend who had made me feel invisible throughout the duration of my treatment.

Although it was lovely to see them, my anxiety was through the roof, as I knew their thoughts and feelings on the whole COVID pandemic - basically, it's nothing worse than the flu, and the death toll has been made up by the government to scare the public into submission. Knowing this, I knew that requesting that a test be taken would fall on deaf ears.

We chatted for some time, me explaining how ill I'd been and how I was lucky to still be here. Hearing this, they broke down and apologised for not being there for me. I foolishly placated them, saying not to worry, you're here now, and no doubt you've had your own problems to deal with.

As they left, I honestly thought that things would be different now. The messaging was again one-sided, with me doing all of the reaching out. For self-preservation, I decided to stop messaging to see if they messaged me first, but it was no surprise that they didn't. Fast forward a few months and they, along with their friendship group, have deleted me on Facebook.

I don't do playground mentality or tactics, and in today's fast-paced culture, Facebook is a great way to keep in touch with people. I think that if you delete someone on Facebook, then you have deleted them from your life.

Realising that I had been deleted not just by a whole friendship group but by one of my main ride-or-die friends hurt me more than they will ever know. At first, I put it down to an error; I know that you cannot possibly delete someone in error, but I was trying to think positive thoughts; after all, the only thing I had done was become ill through no fault of my own. But seeing that more than one person had deleted me made me face the truth that despite everything, I didn't factor into their perfect idea of friendship and lifestyle at all and that they obviously meant more to me than I did to them. When I accepted this, I became angry and upset at the same time, flitting from one emotion to the other quicker than a person suffering from bipolar disorder. I wanted to message them, but I refrained. I then dialled their number but never continued with the call; I wanted to visit them to ask why they had done this, but it wouldn't have changed the fact that they did. Having the answers doesn't change the damage that they have caused. You can't turn the clock back and take away all of the hurt that has been done.

Even now, over a year later, it still hurts. I do not know how I would react if I were to come face-to-face with any of them. Would I cry? Would I be angry? Or would I be so pleased to see them that I would engage in conversation with them? Because they have hurt me so much and because I do not trust what I would do in their presence, I have decided to steer clear.

It is always said that the hardest lessons learned hurt the most. This lesson learnt was incredibly hard. Anyone who has had a cancer diagnosis does not know what the future holds. You hope and pray that the treatment is successful and that the cancer never returns. But with every new symptom, you automatically go to a dark place, thinking that it has.

Because I cannot read tea leaves and look into my future, I grasp every piece of happiness that I can. Any negativity is cut out like the cancer itself. I won't be cliche and say that I live each day like it's my last because if that were true, you would find me on the high-roller tables at a casino whilst taking every single psychedelic drug that I could find - if you are going to go, go out with a bang.

Whilst this lesson was a hard one, another one I have learnt is an amazing one; who my true friends are. They still see me as the person I was pre-cancer, despite the cumbersome aids that I currently need to use. They do not and have never treated me any differently from the moment I first told them that I have cancer. They have taken the piss out of me and have made me laugh until I cry. I sincerely hope that everyone has friends like these because, for me, they have become invaluable.

PICTURES DURING AND AFTER TREATMENT

Pictures during and post-chemotherapy

RACHEL HAYWARD

Like many pastimes, the Paranormal is a strange bedfellow. It brings together people who wouldn't really mingle and challenges the meaning of friendship.

Many people only meet up if they are lucky, once in a blue moon and private lives are rarely discussed.

When I found out about Lisa's BFB, it actually confused me, and I didn't know how to feel. Obliviously, I was shocked and filled with sympathy, but I was unsure of how to react. Should I call, send a 'get well soon' card, or pass on my concerns through a third party? Thankfully Lisa resolved this herself by setting up a private Facebook page and between that and private messaging I realised (albeit a bit late) that it doesn't matter how long you have known someone for or how often you meet or speak, friendship is Friendship whatever the situation.

In situations like this, being open and honest is the best course of action. Dispense with the platitudes and appreciate every second, every laugh , every tear, and every moment of friendship that time gives you.

🖤

Rachel Hayward xxx

TIME TO EVICT THE BEAN-FACED-B*****D

7th March 2023

I was feeling quite stressed when I had to attend my pre-op assessment. I was so worried that the infections, the high heart rate and blood pressure would affect the operation that I was desperate to have.

I am not sure how I would have taken the news if they had said that they would have to postpone my operation. I think that it would have led to my anxiety going into overdrive, which in turn would require more medication to calm me down; either that or I would have had to have been admitted to the nut house/funny-farm/mental health institution, I'll let you take your pick.

A nurse weighs and measures my height. Next, they take some blood samples, including my blood pressure, oxygen levels, and heart rate. My blood pressure and heart rate are high, which I said is to be expected as I have developed 'white coat syndrome'* She made a note of this on my record and said that I was to tell them this on the day of my operation.

She asked me to confirm what operation I was having and why.

OUR LITTLE STAYCATION

11th March 2023

We decided to take some time away between finishing chemotherapy and my operation. As we hadn't seen our family in Devon for some time, we booked a two-night stay at the Saunton Sands Hotel. I used to work here when I was younger, first as a silver service waitress and then as a chambermaid. The hospitality business is hard work, but I found it so rewarding and loved it.

Checking into the hotel, I was conscious of people staring at me; although I wore a hat at all times, having no eyelashes or eyebrows made it perfectly obvious that I was a cancer patient. I was not too fond of people looking at me, realising what was wrong, and then the look in their eyes changing to one of pity or sympathy. Once you have checked in and before they show you to your room, the barman offers you a glass of Prosecco; due to my medications, I could not drink, so Simon was quite pleased that he had two glasses.

One of the staff members showed us to our room. It had double doors that opened onto a balcony overlooking Saunton Sands beach. There was also an adjoining room for Harrison.

Simon moved a chair to the patio doors that led onto the balcony, and I sat there with the doors open, listening to the waves crashing onto the shore and breathing in the smell of the ocean. Oh god, how I'd missed this. I felt instantly calm and relaxed; memories of my childhood flooded. Pointing at different points on the dunes and in the general direction of Saunton Golf Club, I told Harrison tales of my childhood. Suddenly, I felt guilty for moving to a county where we were landlocked and had to travel for nearly an hour to be on the coastline. I believed my children had missed out on everything I enjoyed growing up.

The schools in Devon used to teach about the dangers of the ocean and what to look out for especially underwater currents. It is so easy to be knocked off your feet and then wrapped up in a current that swirls around you and takes you out to sea. I think that they should teach this in schools across the country. You never know; it could one day save someone's life.

During our stay here, we visited a few family members. Unfortunately, we couldn't see all of them as they were unwell, and we couldn't risk me picking up anything so close to my operation.

Simon and I would get up at 7 am each morning and head to the spa, where we would lounge in their Hydropool for an hour or so. It was an infinity pool, with the water disappearing over one edge; the sound of the cascading water had a calming influence on my senses. One wall was entirely glass, so we would watch as the early morning surfers arrived, hoping to catch a big wave.

On our final evening here, after dinner, we returned to our room. I opened the patio doors and listened to the ocean again. Hearing my phone ring, I saw the name of someone I hadn't spoken to in a long time. Answering it, I could instantly tell that she was drunk.

'I'm so angry with you.'

'Why, what have I done?'

'You didn't tell me that you had cancer.'

'I put it on Facebook; I got to the point where I couldn't talk about it anymore.'

'Yes, I saw it the day you posted it. But you should have phoned me and told me that you were dying.'

'I am NOT fucking dying' I hung up and switched my phone to silent. The dark thoughts of an early demise are never far from the forefront of your mind, so having a friend, I use this term

129

loosely, phoning whilst drunk telling me that I am dying really isn't helpful, and it does nothing for my mental health, which is really struggling at the moment.

Unfortunately, our little break ended too soon, and before we knew it, we were packing our things, ready to go home. The anxiety about the operation began as soon as the car engine started for our journey home.

OPERATION DAY

16th March 2023
My operation was initially booked for 14th March, but my surgeon phoned me and asked if I would be willing to move it to today as the Junior Doctors are striking, and she wants to make sure that I receive the best care possible. As her diary was already full for this date, I would need to be operated on by one of her colleagues. If I were to choose to wait until she could operate on me, it would be another four weeks before this could be done. As you can see from the date, I chose not to wait for her. Because, after all, I will be asleep for most of it anyway.

Rachael met Simon and me at the hospital. We had to be there at 8 am, so it was an early start for all three of us.

We checked into the day-patients ward, and after being led to a curtained-off cubicle, my observations were taken; they didn't mention if my heart rate or blood pressure was through the roof, so I assumed that either a) it was okay (nothing short of a miracle), or b) the nurse I saw at my pre-op appointment had made a note that I was suffering from the 'white coat syndrome' on my notes.

The nurse asked if I could be pregnant. At 47 years of age, I sincerely hoped not. We all laughed after Rachael said, 'She'd better not be, or she wouldn't be the only one rocking in the corner'.

The nurse told me that they may still need me to take a pregnancy test, just in case. The powers that be must have decided that it wasn't necessary after all, as a test was never produced.

We make ourselves as comfortable as possible, talking and laughing. Rachael and Simon tried their best to take my mind off the operation. Simon says he hopes I go down before they stop serving breakfast in the Restaurant. Each time I was admitted, we would joke about how his stomach ruled him. He discovered that they would serve Chilli-con-carne each Friday, which is one of his favourites. So you can imagine his disappointment when he went for lunch on Friday, and the menu had been changed. He keeps hoping he'll be there when it is returned to the menu, but it has yet to be. I may have to commission Jamie to make one for him; apparently, he makes a mean one.

A porter came to our little cubicle and told me he had instructions to take me to the Breast Unit. Although the tumour has calcification, a wire guide* will be inserted to ensure that it is easily identifiable during the operation. So, a porter arrives with a wheelchair, and I am wheeled towards the operating theatre while Simon and Rachael wait for me.

The porter is very chatty, which helped distract me from the procedures I needed to have performed today to finally get rid of the 'Bean-Faced-Bastard'.

When he delivered me to the Breast Unit, he bid me farewell and good luck. Once the doctor had completed the procedure, another porter would swing by to take me back to the ward.

I was already wearing a hospital gown, so I didn't need to undress. The nursing staff helped me into the bed and ensured I was comfortable.

Once the local anaesthetic had taken effect, I felt nothing. The wires are guided into place using an ultrasound machine, and I couldn't tell you how many wires were inserted. Whether there was just a single wire to mark the centre of the tumour or if there were more and they were used to mark the margins. They covered the sight of insertion and popped the wire(s) inside, although they didn't stay there, and I would occasionally feel one dig into my upper arm.

The ultrasound technician checked my other breast at the sight where I was sure that I had felt another lump. Paranoia has taken hold, and the slightest thing sends your guts churning with worry that the cancer has spread. She assured me there was nothing to worry about and that she could only see normal breast tissue. Unfortunately, this didn't stop the worrying; I found myself second-guessing if that was the exact location where I had found the lump. For a short time afterwards, I would check the area several hundred times a day, convinced that it had been missed. All I achieved was making the area sore and slightly bruised whilst also giving myself serious mental health issues. I somehow managed to stop doing this, although I am unsure how I did.

Once the ultrasound technician had finished, one of the nurses helped me put the gown back on, off the bed, and back into the wheelchair. The nurse wheeled me back into the waiting room, which, thankfully, was empty of the general public due to the Breast Unit appointments not starting until 9 am. It would be rather embarrassing to be sitting in a room full of people while wearing nothing but a hospital gown to cover your modesty.

A porter arrives quickly and takes me back to the ward, where Rachael and Simon await me.

My surgeon, Chrissie, arrives and asks how I am feeling. Nervous is the only reply that I can think of. She is very caring and tells me not to worry, that she'll look after me.

She asks me to stand in front of her and remove the hospital gown so that she can draw on me. She marks the sight of the tumour, the new placement for my nipple and then where the incisions will be. She turned me around to show Simon and Rachael, asking what they thought. It did make me laugh, especially when she began lifting my boob from behind to show how it should sit once the operation was complete. Simon and Rachael both agreed that it looked good; I'm not sure what their thought process was and whether this was something that they were expecting to be asked. But without a mirror to look in, I trusted their judgement.

Before long, a porter arrived to take me into the operating theatre. I said goodbye to both of them and asked them to make sure that they were both here when I got back. My surgeon told us that the operation should take around two hours, and one of the ward staff gave them a number to call to check how everything was going.

The porter took me to an anti-room, where I had to confirm my name, address, and date of birth again, and I also had to confirm what type of operation I was expecting to have and on what side. The staff checked that the marks that my surgeon had made on my breast were on the correct side and that everything corresponded with the notes. They thoroughly checked that they were about to perform the correct operation on the correct patient. Once they were happy that everything was correct, they wheeled me into an enormous operating theatre. Apart from when I had Harrison by cesarean, which I can't remember much about, I had only ever seen an operating theatre on television. They looked like a broom cupboard in comparison. There was no end of machinery and lights, nurses and doctors buzzing around, making sure that they had everything that they needed.

They asked me to confirm my name, date of birth and the operation I would be having again; the anaesthetists introduced themselves before rendering me unconscious.

I remember being gently woken by a nurse and hearing machinery beep around me. I could hear a lot of beeping, which told me I must have been in the recovery ward and wasn't the only patient there. The medical professional whose task had been to look after me removed the monitors and accompanying bits and bobs, and a porter took me to one of the wards.

The relief on Simon and Rachael's faces was evident. I had been under for over four hours, and they were beginning to worry. especially when you consider that each time they phoned the number to check on my whereabouts, the staff told them they didn't know where I was and that they should call again later.

Once on the ward, two nurses asked me to confirm my name. Although I have no knowledge of this, I said, 'My name is Lisa, but my friends call me twat'. They don't, so I have no idea why I would say this. The nurses found this highly amusing, and when Simon passed the nurse's station a short time later, he found them discussing what I had said with much enjoyment. He responded, 'Yes, that's my wife; I can't take her anywhere.' I think the nurses were slightly concerned about being caught laughing at a patient, but we aren't that precious about ourselves, and if my stupidity can make someone laugh, then I am happy.

The anaesthetic must have been wearing off because I hurt like you wouldn't believe. You would imagine that the incision on my breast would have been the most painful, but it wasn't; the wound underneath my arm was agony. I cannot describe how much it hurt.

My surgeon had warned me that sometimes patients can lose sensation in their upper arm, arm pit, and side where the operation has taken place. This is due to the 'rooting around' they must do to remove the lymph nodes. I was pleased I hadn't lost much sensation here; at least something was going in my favour.

Chrissie, my surgeon, gave me the option to stay overnight, which I took them up on. One, because I hurt like hell, and two, I just want to sleep. Plus, if I am here, Simon doesn't need to worry about me, as he knows I am being taken care of.

The nurses take my observations throughout the night, so sleep is a rare thing. But I managed to drift off quite quickly after each of their visits.

The following morning, the familiar noise of the breakfast and tea trollies woke me as they went about their rounds. I must have still been suffering from the effects of the general anaesthetic as I honestly can't remember what or if I ate anything.

Rachael and Jamie arrived late in the morning to see me. Luckily, they were in time for me to be discharged, so they took me home.

Rachael packed all my things away and helped me get dressed while Jamie waited on the other side of the curtain. As soon as the nurse had shown me how to take care of the drain and what to do if the battery in the negative pressure bandage ran out, Rachael went ahead and brought the car to the front of the hospital.

Jamie carefully wheeled me out of the ward's double doors and towards the hospital's front entrance. I held onto my extremely sore boob the whole way; each time I winced in pain, Jamie was very apologetic. But it was just one of those things, and nothing could be done to help ease the pain.

Climbing into the back of Rachael's car was slightly problematic, one because I was so weak my legs could barely take my weight, and two because every time I moved, the pain became so intense I felt like I would pass out. Luckily, I didn't, and with a lot of help, we managed to crane me into the back of her car. Rachael was very considerate and drove as carefully as possible, not over-accelerating and creating g-force, tempering the brakes slowly and avoiding as many potholes as possible without oversteering. I didn't think she could drive like this, as she is usually very heavy-footed. The thought and care she displayed made me love her even more, and I consider her my best friend. I may not confide everything in her, as there are some things that a mother shouldn't say to her daughter, but I tell her most of the things happening in my life. She is also very good at giving advice and has matured into a level-headed, strong woman. I couldn't be more proud of her. I will never know how I managed to raise this perfect (in my eyes, although I know that I am very biased).

We phoned Simon on our way home to tell him not to come to the hospital, as I was on my way with Rachael and Jamie.

When I got home, it was apparent that Simon was tracking my progress, as he had made a fresh cup of tea and had put clean sheets on the bed in readiness for me.

I was still so exhausted that I went straight to bed. Scaling the stairs with Simon behind me, his hands on my waist, aiding me with each step by giving me a little lift. Rachael wasn't far behind with a cup of tea for me and her. They helped me undress and settle into bed. Rachael sat on the bed next to me, and we chatted until my eyes grew heavy, and I drifted off to sleep.

Apparently, Harrison popped his head around the open door to check if I was okay, although I don't remember this. Considering his age and the stress of trying to study for his A-level exams, I feel Harrison struggled the most. When coming home from school, finding his ordinarily active mum lying on the sofa, barely able to move, must have been difficult for him. Because of the effect the chemotherapy had on my immune system, Harrison became distant, fearing that he would pass on something that could potentially hospitalise me. Harrison is very good at researching things on the internet, and because of this, I do not doubt that he would have spent a significant amount of time researching my cancer and the effects all of the drugs would have on me. He would spend time with Simon in the lounge after I had gone to bed, and they would sit chatting while drinking whiskey. I think they were trying to reassure each other that I would pull through this and be fine.

When I was pregnant with Harrison, I developed Symphysis Pubis Dysfunction* at 15 weeks; anyone who has had this condition will know how debilitating it can be. I spent months walking with crutches or using a wheelchair. I also developed the skill of not moving in my sleep, which was a godsend after my recent operation. I would wake up in the same position which I had fallen asleep in, which minimised the pain. However, having to remember to assemble the drainage bag and the battery pack for the negative pressure dressing was a pain, whether getting into or out of bed.

I spent my days in much the same way as I had during chemotherapy, still being incredibly weak, making daily living a constant battle. I even struggled to pick up cups that were too full, and being able to cut up my food was also out of the question. Simon would have to help me perform everyday tasks that most people take for granted. Some days, I would be too weak to go downstairs, so I would spend the day in bed; whilst awake, I would try to keep my mind occupied by watching television, reading a book, or playing games on my phone.

REMOVAL OF SURGICAL DRAIN

20th March 2023

At some point, Rachael and Simon tried to put the special post-op bra on me, but I was so swollen at this point, and in so much pain we decided to leave it. We phoned the breast unit and told them that we were having problems, asking if they could assist us. So, off to the hospital we go; I have spent so much time here that I refer to it as my favourite five-star hotel. Some of the staff laugh at this, whilst others barely crack a smile.

The lovely breast care nurse managed to wrangle me into the bra. I was quite surprised that the pain in my breast reduced slightly as soon as the bra was put on me, and I felt a slight sense of relief.

Whilst we were there, my surgeon popped in to check on me and to see how I was recovering from the op. She checked how much fluid had collected in the drainage bag and decided the nurse could remove the drain. What happened next, I am sure, has left me scarred.

The drain is a simple tube with a few tiny stitches that keeps it in place and stops gravity from pulling it out. The nurse cut away at the stitches and then told me that removing the tube might hurt slightly as she removed it. Can you guess it? Yep, it wasn't 'slightly painful'. It was excruciating, to the point that I was screaming in pain as if I was giving birth (I can only imagine what these feel like, as both of mine were born through cesareans). The amount of pain that the nurse was putting me through affected her. She stopped and asked if I wanted to continue. I told her to ignore me and get it done. After all, delaying the procedure wouldn't make it hurt any less, and the drain needed to be removed, so it's best to get on with it through gritted teeth.

I couldn't have been happier when she told me the drain was out. She left the room to get me a glass of water and to give me some time to compose myself before wrangling me into the bra again.

Simon held me close, telling me that it's okay now. This man is amazing; he has been by my side the whole time, offering support and making sure that I am as comfortable as possible. I can't think of anyone else I would want to continue battling through life with. He is my best friend, confidante, and soul mate, and he is all rolled into one fantastic human being. I sometimes forget that although I was going through the treatment, he was also going through it alongside me. Most of the time, he would be doing it all alone; Rachael, Harrison and Jamie were great, but I can imagine that any fears Simon may have had that I could possibly not make it through would not be discussed with them.

D-DAY, DID THEY GET IT ALL?

30th March 2023
We arrived at the hospital early, so we had a short amount of time to kill before meeting with my surgeon. We immediately grabbed coffee and cake from the Atrium cafe outside the breast unit. I don't know why I always order a cappuccino, as I really don't like their coffee. I should have stuck to breakfast tea because at least I would have been able to drink it. I took a few cautious sips from the cup, decided that I still didn't like their coffee and pushed it to one side. Simon and I shared a muffin, a tradition that we seem to have started since coming here. I think this is because Simon shouldn't be eating things like this as he has diabetes and because my appetite is practically non-existent, and I would end up wasting most of it.

When we had five minutes to spare before our appointment, we cleared the table and went to the breast unit. Checking in, we waited in the busy waiting room. It wasn't long before a nurse called my name, and we dutifully followed the nurse to a reasonably sized office. My surgeon, Chrissie, was there wearing a big smile on her face. In that instant, I couldn't decide if she was smiling because it was good news or if the smile was a way of settling my anxiety and lulling me into a false sense of security.

Sitting next to her, she informed me that the cancer was gone. They had removed good margins of healthy tissue around the tumour, and she was pleased to tell me that only two lymph nodes were affected. I can now say that I am cancer-free.

The relief we both felt must have shown. I told her I could hug her as tears of joy ran down my face. She offered me a tissue and asked if she could check the wound site for how I was healing.

Inspecting the scar, she was pleased with how everything looked. I tell her that it's weird looking down at my chest now;

one side is the breast of a seventeen-year-old, whilst the other is my actual age of Forty-seven. I can have the 'old breast' operated on to make it the same size as the 'new' one. They will call me back in approximately six months if I choose to have this done. The size difference is so significant that I elect to proceed with this procedure.

Leaving the hospital, we are in shock; we've done it! We got through it! The cancer has gone! If I could skip, I definitely would have done it.

Getting back to the car, Simon helped me stand, and we held each other tightly before he helped me into the car. We decided to go to our favourite Italian Restaurant in the centre of Bath. Unfortunately, it has closed now. To celebrate the results, we decided to forget the expense; this was worth celebrating.

Simon wheeled the chair to the back of the car. I heard him grunt, and then there was nothing. He was at the back of the car, and I couldn't hear anything from him. I couldn't leave the car unaided or turn around to see if he was okay. Fearing the worst, I began to panic. My heart began to beat faster, and my breathing quickened; it felt as if my heart was about to explode out of my chest, like a scene from Alien. He had my bag and phone, and I felt as if I were trapped in the car, unable to help him.

I was on the verge of a full-blown panic attack when I heard a woman's voice and then Simons's response to her. Thank god, he was okay. My heart rate and breathing began to slow and return to normal.

Simon opened the door and slowly climbed into the driver's seat, wincing in pain. He saw my state of panic and told me that he twisted funny and pulled his back out whilst trying to lift the wheelchair into the boot of the car. The woman's voice I heard was her offering to help him put it in the car. Faith in humanity was restored slightly by this kind passer-by offering assistance, whilst a few members of the public had passed him by, looking at him leaning over the bin in obvious pain.

ENDOCRINE TREATMENT

19th April 2023

The past few weeks passed in a blur. It was lovely not to have to go to the hospital for treatment or admission for infections; you could actually forget about the nightmare we were currently living. But there was still the flurry of letters for future appointments that would land on the doormat regularly, making you realise with a jolt that there were still further treatments and hospital appointments to go through.

We are back at the hospital to discuss the next part of my treatment.

Because I am pre-menopausal and because my cancer is hormone-positive, I need to have my ovaries switched off. To achieve this, I have to take a pill daily pill - Letrozole, and also have a twelve-weekly injection - Prostap. The course of this treatment is five years.

I have been taking the Letrozole for a few weeks now, so it is well and truly in my system. Today is the first of the injections. I also have to take a drug called Abemacyclib. We are informed of the side effects, which are almost the same as the ones I endured whilst going through chemotherapy, although not quite as severe. The fact that it would also weaken my immune system bothered me, and that I would need to take it for two years. Because of the damage that the medication can do to your body, for the first three months, you have to have fortnightly blood tests done to check how your body is coping. Then, the blood samples need to be taken every four weeks; it is the patient's responsibility to ensure that the bloods are taken in time so that the results are back ready for the release of the next prescription.

As the nurse is not qualified to inject in my arm, she has to administer it in my leg. So I have to try my hardest to get out of the wheelchair, stand up, and remove my trousers so that this can be done. Simon was unable to help me as the cubicle was so small that there was barely room for myself and the nurse. With a good amount of determination, the prostap was administered, and I was free to go.

ACUPUNCTURE

1st May 2023

Simon had done some research into the effectiveness of acupuncture on the condition that the extensive treatment has left me with.

There is a little shop in the centre of town called 'Dr China' that offers an acupuncture service. Simon popped in to see if they felt that they would be able to help me. He called to check if it was something that I wanted to try, and then he made an appointment for the following week.

I was quite nervous about what to expect when I attended my first appointment. It didn't help that the older Chinese man who greeted us barely spoke English. So, with blind faith again, I assumed the position required for the treatment to take place.

I have previously mentioned that I am a seamstress and have been for most of my life, so I am used to pricking myself with needles and pins. So, it would be safe to assume that I wouldn't find this procedure painful. It was marginally painful, and then it became uncomfortable. Needles were placed in my scalp, down my spine, behind my ears, and across both hips. When the needles were placed in my scalp, I could hear a crackling sound, as if the needle were going through gristle.

I had about five of these treatments in total, but due to the cost, I had to stop. Because of my drastic decline, Simon stopped working soon after my surgery to become my full-time carer, so finances were becoming strained.

At one acupuncture appointment, the therapist was humming to himself while inserting the needles. I joked that he was enjoying it far too much. His response was excellent, hinting at the humour hidden below the surface: 'Ha ha, and you pay for it!' Imagine it being said in the same tone as the Chinese actor in one of the Lethal Weapon films. I can't remember which one now, but I think the character was called Benny.

We would always treat ourselves to a shake-away afterwards, which is obviously shared. We would take it in turns as to who would choose the flavour.

CRAIG WILLIAMS

I met Lisa through my paranormal friend Karin. We ended up on a few investigations together, and later on in the same team at the Jamaica Inn, hosting paranormal nights.

Lisa has a huge character and is always up for a laugh, particularly with her partner in crime Karin. Together they are often my worst nightmare.

Lisa, Karin and I also now work together in my business, so I've got to know Lisa a lot better over the years.

When Lisa got her diagnosis, I was blown away by her pragmatism and positivity.

She's been an absolute inspiration to me in her outlook and in her relationship with the circumstances that occurred.

She has been my teacher.

Craig Williams

A POEM BY LISA

My Poor Neglected Friends
by Lisa Holman

To My poor neglected Friend, I'm sorry

If you feel I neglected you then I'm sorry

If you feel unsupported, I'm sorry

If you feel unloved and I'm sorry

If I ever made you feel invisible, then I'm sorry

I'm sorry that I became ill

I'm sorry that to be able to deal, you neglected me.

I'm sorry that to be able to deal, you were unable to support me.

I'm sorry, that to be able to deal, you made me feel unloved

I'm sorry that in your eyes, I became invisible.

One day, perhaps you will find the courage to say sorry to me

WELCOME TO THE WORLD LITTLE MAN

10th May 2023
We received a phone call from Jamie, who told us that Rachael was in labour. I was so excited--I was going to be a Nan, and I couldn't wait to meet my Grandson!

To prove how f****d up my body is, I managed to damage my shoulder whilst moving in bed a few days prior to this. I don't quite know how I managed it, but I did.

It's Wednesday again, which means Tash is coming over. Going through treatment and having to isolate yourself is tough. It also meant that Tash couldn't come around. She works in an office, and there are always people popping in and out. You could never tell if someone was carrying something but was symptomatic. So, to keep me safe, she steered clear of me. We talked occasionally on the phone if I was awake and had the energy, but she spoke frequently with Simon.

My shoulder hurt so much that I couldn't eat the dinner they had prepared. I took some painkillers and decided that the best place to be would be in bed. Climbing the stairs with one arm out of action was extremely difficult, but again, my hero hubby and Tash helped me all the way.

Sitting on the bed, topless, they both look at my shoulder from all angles and compare it to the other one. Considering the amount of pain that I was in, they decided to call for help.

The paramedic who arrived was very kind. He did his best to inspect my shoulder, but even the slightest touch or movement would be excruciating and make me whimper. Because the shoulder that I had injured was on the same side as the cancer and my operation, he decided to call for advice on the best treatment. He gave us two choices: one, wait for an ambulance to transport me, which could be a few hours and may not even arrive until the next day, or two, make our way to the hospital.

He would advise them that I was on my way, so I should be seen relatively quickly. We chose option two.

The ambulance man helped me out of the house and secured me in the car, and then we were off to the hospital yet again.

Arriving at the Accident and Emergency Department, we were whisked straight into a cubicle. Because of my weakened immunity, the nursing staff are always eager to keep me away from other patients in case they pass on something to me.

A nurse tried his best to examine me and then sent me for an X-ray, as he couldn't tell what I'd done to myself.

The X-ray is done. I am taken back to the cubicle to wait on the results. We phone Jamie to tell him what is happening in case Rachael decides to track us. Although we knew that she was indisposed, we decided that it would be better to let them know so that Rachael wouldn't panic while in labour.

Sometime later, the nurse came back to my cubicle and told me that I had bone burrs on my shoulder joint, the movement I made in bed managed to dislodge one, and it caused inflammation. I have to wear a sling to remove pressure on the joint whilst it repairs itself. The nurse also prescribes anti-inflammatories to help speed up the healing process and hopefully remove some of the pain.

Putting the sling on was awful; the nurse tried his best to create as little movement and pain as possible. He told me that if I felt the need to swear to go ahead, my 'fuck-a-duck' caused him to laugh and tell me that he hadn't heard that one before.

I'M A NAN!

We were waiting for the pharmacy to dispense my prescription when Simon showed me a photo of a chubby, red-faced brand new baby boy. He had lots of dark hair, and he looked perfect. He screwed up his little eyes and clenched his fists as he became aware of this new world that he now inhabits.

The moment I'd been waiting for since they had announced the pregnancy was here, I'm a Nan, and my heart melted. I felt the same instant love that I had felt after meeting my own two children for the very first time. We were both smiling uncontrollably and must have looked like Cheshire cats as we left the hospital.

I couldn't wait to meet him and congratulate Rachael and Jamie in person, but Simon and I had agreed to wait until they were ready to take visitors. Becoming parents for the first time can be a shock to the system, and the sleepless nights that a newborn infant invariably brings mean that you need time to acclimatise yourself. Although you want to show off this little bundle you have created and nurtured, you must rest as much as possible.

We finally got to see him when he was a few days old. Although I wanted to rush straight over as soon as they got home, I was extremely patient and waited until we were given the all-clear that they were ready for visitors.

Rachael was surprised we were waiting for their say-so when we spoke to her a few days later. We went straight around, and the journey felt like it took forever. I swear that Simon was driving so slowly that even James May could have beaten him. We eventually pulled up outside their house, and again, Simon took forever to gather his things. Due to my mobility issues, I was using a wheely walker (or a rollator for most people), so I could not get out of the car without assistance. Patience is not usually a virtue that I hold; however, since my diagnosis and then my gradual decline, it is a trait that I have had to learn. I could have quickly become angry and aggressive if I hadn't, which is definitely not the kind of person I would want to become.

We went into their lounge to see Jamie holding his son. At this point, they still hadn't given him a name. They couldn't agree on one throughout the pregnancy, so I advised them to meet him first, as sometimes the name selected didn't fit the child born. Each day, his name changed until they could decide on a name that worked for him. Jamie looked pleased as punch and so proud of this little life they had created.

Sitting in the corner of the sofa, my Grandson was placed gently into my arms. I was still incredibly weak, so cushions were wedged underneath my arm to help me to support his weight. I couldn't help but stare at him, taking in all of his features, from his dark head of hair to his little button nose and his hands with perfect little fingers and fingernails, still clenched into fists. I stroked his hair in wonder at how beautiful he was and that he was the little miracle that made me keep fighting, determined that I would get to meet him and that he would grow up knowing who Simon and I were. I also knew that if it hadn't been for Rachael's pregnancy, she would have probably gone off the rails and begun to drink heavily.

When it was time to feed him, I didn't want to pass him back, so I gave him his bottle and winded him. Becoming a grandparent is like riding a bicycle; you never forget what to do.

I could have stayed there forever, revelling in holding him. But it was time to leave, so we arranged to pop around later in the week. Throughout Rachael's pregnancy, I told Simon that I wanted our Grandson to know who we were, to be present in his life, and to see him at least once a week. Apart from the odd holiday, we have managed to do it.

When he was about a week old, Rachael and Jamie told us that they had settled on the name Frankie, or Fat Frank, as he is sometimes affectionately called. This nickname will stop soon, as we wouldn't want him to get a complex. He isn't fat, just extremely chunky. He has rolls in all the right places.

We video call each other every day, and Frankie has gotten used to the sound of the ringtone now. His little face lights up when he sees me but lights up even more when he sees Simon. When he was little, I sang 'ba, ba, babarino' to him. We couldn't understand why he always said Ba when he saw me. Eventually, the penny dropped, so I stopped singing this. He now calls me nan-nan, which warms my heart.

Stressful times aside, I loved being a parent. But being a nan is so much better; it doesn't involve stress. You don't need to worry about whether or not the way you are raising your child will have lasting implications into adulthood; there is no need to worry about how secure your job is and what would happen were you to lose it. You can enjoy your time with them, watching them grow and learn new skills or words. I will be forever thankful to Rachael, one for making me a mum and two for making me a nan.

RADIOTHERAPY TREATMENT

28th April 2023
To help align me with the radiotherapy machine, I have to attend a private clinic in Bristol to have three tiny dots tattooed on me. One dot is tattooed on my breastbone, and the others are placed on either side of my upper torso. The procedure is relatively painless, although I was expecting the tattoos to be applied with a tattoo gun of the type found in tattooist parlours. Instead, the nurse makes a small nick in the skin, applying ink to the area.

You are laid down on a hard metal slab with various holes and measurements. The holes are used to place different pieces of equipment to manoeuvre you into position while also trying to keep you as comfortable as possible while supporting you. The equipment and measurements are noted on your file, which will be sent to the hospital. Each time you attend for radiotherapy, they use these notes to ensure that you are placed in the same position each time.

RADIOTHERAPY BEGINS

12th May 2023

The oncology department has decided that I will need ten rounds of radiotherapy, which is administered every weekday. Although the actual radiotherapy treatment doesn't take very long, it takes longer to move you into position and set the machine up than the treatment itself.

Checking in at reception, I notice that there are a lot of people in the confined waiting room, so my anxiety begins to hit the roof; I try taking deep breaths to calm myself down. Luckily, a nurse called my name soon after we had arrived at the unit, so I didn't need to hang around the waiting area for long. The nurse showed us to a changing room with two doors, one of which we had just come through and another internal one, which I assumed led to the treatment room. The nurse instructed me to remove my upper garments and pop a hospital gown on. They would knock on the internal door when they were ready for me.

As my shoulder was still really painful, trying to manoeuvre my arm into the position that it needed to be in was problematic, and the nurses were worried about causing more damage if they were to force it. Using an extraordinary amount of sticky tape, they managed to get me into position and move any of the flesh on my arm out of the way.

The staff asked if I was comfortable, and I answered yes. Even though I wasn't, the nurses left the room while the radiotherapy treatment was being given.

It took less than five minutes to complete the treatment, which seemed to pass in the blink of an eye. Once it was finished, they called Simon in to help me off the bed and back into the wheelchair. We make our way back to the changing room. Once I change into my everyday clothes, we place the hospital gown in the laundry bin and make our way to the hospital restaurant. It is Friday, and Simon hopes they have Chilli-con-carne on the menu. Unfortunately, they didn't, so he had to choose something else. At the initial appointment to discuss the radiotherapy treatment, the oncologist warned me that the therapy could sometimes cause burning and blistering to the skin; if this were to happen, they would supply a cooling gel pad that could be worn inside your bra. Due to the closeness to your lungs, research suggests that it can also cause lung cancer. Again, the oncologist tells us what symptoms to look out for if this happens. So far (fingers crossed), so good.

RADIOTHERAPY CONSULTATION

24th May 2023

As part of my treatment involves putting me into premature menopause, there is the fear that I could develop osteoporosis. With this in mind, we were invited to a consultation with a doctor to discuss the medication required to prevent this.

I never really used to pay attention to the rarer side effects of medication, but you can bet your bottom dollar that I look at every single side effect now.

We are starting with the most common side effects related to taking Bisphosphonates.

Nausea - fatigue - constipation or diarrhoea. These side effects I can deal with as they have become commonplace in my life since starting my treatment.

Moving onto the rarer side effects

Blood supply to your jaw bone dies - leading to breakages

Blood supply to your inner ear bones dies - leading to deafness.

Shattering, not a simple break, a shattering of the thigh bone.

These I am less able to deal with; all I could do was picture myself as a deaf-mute who was unable to move.

Simon began laughing when the doctor read off the list of possible side effects. I remember looking at him and thinking that he was being incredibly rude.

When the doctor responded, 'I'm not really selling this to you, am I?' The words she had spoken began to sink in. I realised then that if Simon had not been in the room questioning the use of this medication, I would have agreed to take it.

The upshot is that we didn't even know if I needed to take it or not since I hadn't had a bone density (DEXA) scan, but the consultants wanted me to start this medication practically immediately.

We opted to have a bone scan done first and then discuss our options if the results indicated that I was at risk of developing osteoporosis.

I am pleased to say that when the results came back, my bone health was determined to match my age; woohoo! There is no need to take any more nasty medication.

FINAL RADIOTHERAPY TREATMENT

26th May 2023

Today is my last radiotherapy, and it marks the end of the whirlwind of treatment schedules, hospital appointments and admissions.

At times, I didn't think I would get here, so saying that I was feeling emotional would be an understatement.

We had planned for Rachael, Frankie and Jamie to be there to watch me ring the bell that would mark the end of my treatment. My dad also planned on travelling from North Devon to support and watch me do this.

Unfortunately, they could not attend due to illness, but Simon videoed and sent it to them.

SARAH DEVERILL

Okay. So, Lisa said she would like us to write a piece about her little group of friends who knew of her illness and her support network.

Having lost a few friends to the dreaded C word, and having friends who are still fighting, when Lisa told us about her fight and her support group, I was happy to join in. To say Lisa has a very different sense of humour to me would be true. She wanted insults and something to make her laugh. We had Karin who was certainly on top form on the insults. I am a little more reserved than some, so for me it was about making sure Lisa was doing okay, the occasional word of encouragement and the occasional insult or joke!

Funnily I knew Lisa would fight this with all her heart. In life you get those who have that fighting spirit and Lisa had this in abundance. Lisa certainly has had some very deep and troublesome times. We may not hear from her for a day or two but when she was back, she was back with a vengeance. I have watched her journey and knew she would fight long and hard, with her proton pack on her back and her Scooby snacks at hand!!!

Unfortunately, she still has a way to go on her journey and I am glad to say I will be there for her as long as she needs me to. Our friendship is still quite new, having met because of our hobby of paranormal investigation. God she can be so loud sometimes! But that is Lisa, and we wouldn't have her any other way.

Onwards and upwards.

WE DID IT!!

Well, we did it!

We got to the end, we are finally here and the treatment is finished.

The endless hospital appointments are over, except for a yearly mammogram and then the maintenance medication. We got here; we did it, and we got through despite every hurdle we had placed in our way and every cog that fate put in the works. We got over it all, but now what?

Where do we go from here? It's a bit of an anticlimax.

The relief that we got to the end is overwhelming, but our lives have been filled with appointments for treatment, taking medication, and constantly monitoring the symptoms and my temperature. Where do we go from here? I can tell you where we go from here; we fill our lives to the brim.

We carry on making plans and act on the plans that we have already made for the future.

We fill our lives with memories, spending time with family and friends, and loving each other.

If you have someone in your life who you think the world of, tell them. Tell people what they mean to you because you may not get a chance tomorrow.

MAINTENANCE MEDICATION

2nd June 2023
We are at the hospital again, this time to discuss the maintenance medication that I will need to take for the next five years.

The oncologist tells me the name of the medication, and I ask why it's changed. The breast care nurses said to me on numerous occasions that I would be taking Tamoxifen. They even gave me a leaflet explaining what the medication was, what it was used for, and all the side effects were listed.

The oncologist was surprised that the breast unit had told me that I would be prescribed Tamoxifen and that it had been decided that I would be taking Abemacyclib.

As the medication can impact kidney and liver function, she explained that I would need to have fortnightly blood tests taken for two months and then once every four weeks. I would also receive a four-weekly phone call from an oncologist, so I would need to make sure that the results were back in time for this. They monitor you very closely while you are on this medication.

I'm not sure if it is because the side effects can be horrendous or if it is because it is a relatively new drug in the fight against cancer.

DEXA SCAN

7th June 2023

We are at the hospital again, this time for a relatively quick procedure, but I am still dreading it. To clarify, I am not dreading the actual procedure; I am dreading the results. I really don't want to have to take a medication that has so many awful side effects. It's strange because before this happened, I never really paid attention to the 'more uncommon, really uncommon' side effects listed on the patient information leaflets. But with everything that has happened recently, I am paying closer attention to these side effects than before.

The patient information leaflet explaining the procedure asks that you wear loose clothing with no metallic objects on your trousers, so anything with a zip is out. I carefully selected a pair of black jersey culottes. They had an elasticated waist with a drawcord, so no zips were in sight.

When I checked in at the department, a nurse took us into a small room; there was barely enough room for Simon, me, and my rollator. There is a curtained-off area opposite the door, and a nurse pulls it back, telling me that they won't be long, and asks me to fill out a consent form. Because I struggle with understanding things, Simon filled it out, and I signed it. They check my height, which throughout my adult life I thought was 5ft 4"; I actually measure 5ft 2". So either I have been wrong the whole time or shrunk 2". I'm going with the fact that I was wrong, as I am not tall enough to be shrinking already.

The problem with being short is that climbing onto most medical beds can be difficult. So, with Simon on one side of me and a nurse on the other, we managed to get me onto the scanner. The medical staff then asked Simon to leave the room while the nurse moved me into position. Ideally, she would have wanted to remove my shoes, but when I explained that, it would cause a great deal of pain. I would have happily removed them if it was strictly necessary, but they kindly agreed that I could keep them on, which was a great relief for me.

A pleather-covered triangular foam pad is placed underneath my knees, placing my legs at an angle to my hips. The nurses disappear behind a protective screen, and the imaging begins. Another pad is placed beneath my knees, making my legs ninety degrees from my hips; again, the nurse disappears behind her protective screen, ready for the scanner to take the images. I look over to them as it is taking a lot longer this time, I can make out the confusion on their faces. One of the nurses approached me, asking if I had any metal objects on my lower half or if I had any metal implants at all. Checking my trousers, we discovered that the hole that the drawstring comes out of is a metal eye. So, despite my care in choosing the correct item of clothing, I was still wearing metal. We managed to slip my trousers down slightly to take the image.

As soon as they had taken all of the images that they needed, they called Simon back in to help me off the bed. He is so used to what is required to move me around now that it is easier to get him to help than to explain to someone what help is needed.

I am exhausted; even the most menial tasks can completely wipe me out. So I sit on the rollator, and Simon pushes me back to the main entrance, via the restaurant, of course. After he had eaten his fill, I just had a pudding and barely managed to eat any of that. We left the hospital and headed home, where I went straight to bed. I slept through the night, waking early the following morning.

SABRINA PRICE

From the instant I met Lisa, I knew she was my cup of tea!!!!!

A great dirty mind, a sense of humour, and a personality like a bottle of pop, which I love.

Over the years, we have had many chats and shared messages, as well as attending paranormal investigations, which Lisa has a passion for.

Then the sad news came that Lisa had cancer; she fought all the way with her cracking sense of humour, with myself and other friends taking the piss, Lisa loved this, and it kept her going.

We often talked about her getting rainbow hair, to go with her crazy personality, it's not happened yet, but I'm sure it will soon,

Lisa came out at the end, still with a smile on her face, coming back on investigations with her crutches, walking up and down stairs, enjoying every moment, one occasion, I jumped out on her, and she nearly fell over. HA HA!!!!!

Lisa's words were you fucking bitch, laughing her head off!!!

This is Lisa, she's one of the most incredible ladies I have ever met in my life, beautiful inside and out and full of fun and craziness and has a dirty mind, so inspirational for writing books too,

I'm proud to call this lady a very special friend of mine.

Love ya mate xxx

QU STUDIOS

11th June 2023

When the Coaching Inn Group bought the Jamaica Inn in 2022, Karin and I travelled to meet the then CEO Kevin Charity at the White Swan in Wells a few months later. The outcome of this meeting was that we would contact the rest of the hotels in the Group's property portfolio to ascertain whether they could successfully hire out the venue for the paranormal. We also passed along the details for Qu Studios in Bristol, which the fabulous Matt and Chris run. We affectionately refer to them as 'The Boys'. Kevin expressed an interest in revitalising the tired museum and having a new, more on-topic video playing in the 'Stable Block'.

Unfortunately, as I was diagnosed a short time after this initial meeting, contacting the other Inns and Hotels was put on the back burner. I did mention to Karin that she should just go ahead without me and that I could advise in the background, but she refused, saying that it wouldn't be the same without me.

The planning of the new video went ahead, with Karin organising interviews and filming schedules. She really is a marvel at how she can bring people together. I joke with her that she is a stalker and needs to put people down.

Matt from Qu Studios has a fantastic talent for mimicking people's mannerisms and voices. Karin, Matt and Chris had been to the Jamaica Inn to interview the manager, Kate, and some other people for the new film. On their way home, back to Bristol, Karin called me so I could say hello to 'The Boys'. Matt began mimicking Andy and Lou from Little Britain; he had me in stitches. He then moved on and began to impersonate the rest of the cast. I laughed so much that my jaw, stomach, and ribs ached like you wouldn't believe it. It was definitely the medicine that I needed, for a few days afterwards; whenever I thought back to this, I would start laughing all over again.

Karin said that the plan was to interview some of the paranormal team members for the film, that I would be interviewed for the video, and that 'the boys' and Karin would do whatever they could to ensure I felt safe while I was in the Studio. Because I was so ill whilst going through my treatment, my interview for the film was put on hold until I was well enough to attend. Again, I told Karin not to worry about me being on it, but she was adamant. The thought of many people passing through the museum looking at my ugly mug wasn't something I was particularly keen on, but Karin is not one to have her mind changed easily.

Once my strength had returned significantly Simon drove me to the Studio for my interview. Craig is one of my paranormal friends, part of the Jamaica Inn paranormal team, and now my boss was also in attendance. I need to mention a few things about Craig: he is a wonderful human being with an amazingly kind soul. Not only does Craig own an accountancy company, but he is also a paranormal investigator, coastguard volunteer, first responder for the ambulance service, surfer (the whiter the waves, the better), and rock climber. Basically, some of his hobbies are the adrenaline junky variety; for this reason alone, Karin calls him 'action man'. He is also a qualified yoga instructor and teaches mindfulness through meditation; through these, he has helped me immensely, and with his guidance, I am trying to accept the here and now.

Everyone is super friendly, and I feel my anxiety begin to settle; it doesn't go completely - it never does, but it has settled significantly enough for me to be able to resemble a normal human being if that has ever been possible where I am concerned.

After saying our hellos, Craig takes his seat in front of the camera, with Karin seated to the right of it to give something for Craig to focus on. Looking down the lens of a camera isn't a good thing, and some people can find it unnerving. Karin reels off her questions, and Craig answers them all, giving some intriguing insights into his time at the Inn.

I am glad Craig went first, giving me time to breathe and try to formulate an intelligent response to the questions. My brain still hadn't returned to the land of the living, so even though I had this extra time to think of my answers, I knew full well that when I sat down in front of the camera, I wouldn't remember them.

Craig whizzed through his questions quickly, so before I knew it, he had finished and said his goodbyes to everyone. I think he was off to 'The Wave' in Bristol with his son. I am tempted to go there one day to have a look. According to Craig, they sometimes do an accessibility session, which would be fantastic for me.

Now it's my turn to sit in front of the camera. I am so nervous that my heart is racing. I try to focus on taking long, slow breaths to calm myself down. Luckily, this works, and I am able to talk without sounding breathless or faltering on my words.

Karin began asking her questions, and surprisingly, I was able to give coherent answers. As soon as I started talking, I couldn't stop, so my answers were probably really long-winded. Luckily, with Chris and Matt's fantastic editing skills, I don't look like a blithering idiot, which is a great feat in itself.

When I had finished answering all of Karin's questions, it was time for us to swap places and tops, as Karin had forgotten to wear her Jamaica Inn one. I added a few relevant questions and a few not-so-relevant ones to make us laugh - 'Karin, can you tell me why you insist on talking to strangers?' 'Is there any way that we can stop you from talking?' Laughter is the key to life, as far as I am concerned.

I'm not entirely sure how it happened, but I am now sitting in front of the camera again. Karin instructed me to tell her about the Facebook page that I had set up, 'Living with Cancer - Trowbridge and the surrounding area'. I set up this page after realising that there isn't really a support network in the town for cancer patients, survivors and family or friends thereof. Admittedly, since setting it up, I haven't had the time to organise anything. Although I have a lot of plans for it, but at the moment, it has stagnated while I concentrate on other projects.

What followed was the most cathartic release that I have ever experienced. I opened up completely and gave an honest insight into how some friends drifted away. Because they didn't know how to react, not just to my diagnosis but also to the treatment and my ever-changing appearance, they didn't react; first, a day goes past, then a week, then a month, and then it's too late. I hadn't realised until this point how deeply it had affected me; losing friends when you need them the most really does cut you to the core. Although I know that their coping mechanism of ignoring me wasn't intentional, the damage has been done, and the past cannot be rewritten. I'm not sure if it is something that I will ever be able to forgive. Chris did another fantastic job editing the video for me, and under Karin's instruction, I posted it on my Facebook and TikTok pages; everyone who took the time to watch it had a great response, which I found embarrassing and overwhelming. Because I am not the kind of person who airs my life on social media, most people didn't realise how poorly I had become during my treatment. Being told by several people that I am an inspiration is exceptionally humbling and not something I can accept; I just faced each day as it came, thankful for still being here.

PROBLEMS WITH MAINTENANCE

14th June 2023
The medication that I needed to take came with awful side effects; the one I was most concerned about was weakened immunity. The one that caused me the most problems was the severe diarrhoea. I won't go into detail, but suffice it to say that even with the medication to help stop this side effect, there were some days when I dared not leave the bathroom, let alone the house.

A phone call with my oncologist confirmed that they wouldn't regard this as quality of life. So, I am advised to stop taking the medication for a few days, giving time for my stomach to settle. They will then reintroduce it at a lower dose.

20th June 2023
So, I am back on the medication that has caused me too many problems. My anxiety has been through the roof, knowing that I need to start retaking them, and I am hoping that the reduced dose helps to stop the awful side effects that I have experienced.

Even after the dose had been reduced by a third, I still experienced the same side effects, but not quite as severe. The medication was reduced a second time, and with the support medication, I was able to have some form of life. But knew that I shouldn't go far from a bathroom. This made any long journeys particularly troublesome.

RETURNING TO THE PARANORMAL

Throughout this whole relentless journey, from diagnosis to finishing the core part of my treatment, it is my paranormal friends who have stuck by my side. When you consider most of them, we barely know each other; we may meet up a few times a year to investigate a venue. The amount of time we spend together to discuss everyday life is conducted during the breaks and is so tiny compared to the amount of time spent in the dark calling out for something to happen. So I think that these people are absolutely remarkable!

Thanks to the majority of the paranormal television shows, or 'ooh, it's a demon' shows, the paranormal community has faced a lot of backlash, and some individuals frequently mock this hobby. As with everything in life, there are significant divides. Some are after turning a fast buck by faking evidence, and some live stream while breaking into a supposedly abandoned building, failing to realise that just because the property has been abandoned, it doesn't mean someone doesn't own it.

There are also those investigators who have integrity and are trying their hardest to enlighten the paranormal community. They have a solid moral compass and treat each venue and whatever inhabits its fibres with respect. I am lucky to be a part of this section of the community. We hang our heads in shame when we see what the 'get rich quick' section posts online.

The people I investigate regularly with are part of several teams, and we all have different philosophies, beliefs, and ways of investigating. There is never any animosity, and we all rub along really well and try different things. Some things work, and some don't, but it's the trying that matters.

I had really missed seeing these friends, some of whom I hadn't seen since September 2022. I couldn't wait to return to the paranormal world.

THE TALBOT HOTEL - OUNDLE

17th April 2023 - As part of our agreement with The Coaching Inn Group to approach their property portfolio and help them maximise profits from hiring their venue out to the paranormal community, we decided that the first hotel we would tackle would be The Talbot Hotel in Oundle. Some have reported that Mary Queen of Scots haunts this beautiful coaching inn. The stone facade was composed of reclaimed stones from the nearby Fotheringhay Castle, where Mary met her untimely demise at the hands of an executioner.

Karin picked me up bright and early, as we had a good two and a half hours to travel. My emotions are all over the place. I am excited and nervous all at once.

I am excited because I am finally coming back to the paranormal. I will get to meet Lorien for the first time, investigate an amazing location, and spend time with Karin, who has been an absolute godsend.

I am nervous because I will need to rely heavily on Karin and Lorien to get me up and down the stairs, cut up my food, dress me, undress me, and help me take my medication.

I have shared rooms with Karin for years, and getting dressed and undressed in front of her has never been an issue. But having to ask her to perform these tasks for me is embarrassing. You may have already been able to tell that I am independent and strong-willed, so handing over complete autonomy was very difficult for me. Travelling with Karin is never dull. We laugh until we cannot breathe. Our sense of humour centres around insulting each other, which some of our friends think is rude but we find incredibly funny.

We laughed the entire journey, given that my brain still hadn't fully recovered. I don't know why she listened to me when I told her to ignore the satnav and go in the direction that I thought was correct, even considering that I have no sense of direction and could get lost in a brown paper bag. We had to turn around quite a few times, which was hysterical.

Exiting the car, we discovered that I had completely seized up, and my feet felt non-existent, so we decided it would be a good idea if I sat on my wheels and Karin would push me. Now, my brain takes a while to understand what is happening around it, and sometimes, most of what is happening makes no sense to me at all. Obviously, this is excellent material for Karin, and she excels in taking the mick and making me laugh. The position of the seat and handles meant I was being pushed backwards down a gradual incline; although I knew that I was safe with Karin and that she wouldn't let go of me, my brain would not stop my fear. I held onto Karin's wrists for dear life. She laughed the whole time at me, joking that she would let go.

The hotel staff were terrific. They were very accommodating and didn't make me feel disabled at all. There was some concern over whether I could scale the two flights of Jacobean stairs to our rooms, but I assured them that it might take me a while, but I would definitely be able to do it.

We made our way to the lounge area and ordered a hot drink each; they came with a little shot glass filled with malteasers; how amazing! Lorien arrived shortly after us; ordering a drink, we settled in and chatted. Have you ever met someone for the first time and felt you have known them your entire life? Lorien is one of these people; the minute she sat opposite me, I felt we had known each other since birth. I have been lucky to experience this a few times in my life, and I sincerely hope you have also experienced this, as the feeling is exceptionally calming.

A staff member named Josh introduced himself and said that he and another staff member would be joining us for the evening's investigation. He was quite jittery and explained that he had witnessed a few things. We told him not to divulge it until the end of the evening as it is possible to implant an idea in someone's head without them realising it, and then their brain makes it real for them.

Josh offered to show us around the hotel, but due to my mobility issues and the venue being a few hundred years old and listed, there are no lifts, so I decided to stay put while Karin and Lorien were shown the different areas. When we visit a new venue, it is important to work out vigil areas that won't impact the public who are also staying at the hotel.

We arranged to meet up with Josh after we had eaten our evening meal, which I have to say the food was terrific.

At the beginning of the investigation, Josh was extremely skittish and nervous; at the end, his demeanour had changed completely. He was no longer fearful of what may still reside within the walls of the hotel. This is the effect some of the paranormal shows have on people; we see it all the time at the Jamaica Inn.

With the investigation finished, it was time to climb the mountain of stairs to our rooms. But I was exhausted. My legs refused to work, and I couldn't feel my feet or hands at all, except for the sharp razor blade pain that would shoot up them if they came into contact with anything.

Getting me up the stairs was a mammoth task. The night porter even had to lend a hand. With Karin's finger in the belt loop of my jeans, the night porter on the other side of me, and Lorien bringing up the rear, quite literally, we did it.

Lorien moved my left foot onto the step, making sure that it was flat, then Karin and the night porter pulled me up, with Lorien moving my right foot, once again making sure that it was flat. It took forever; my legs kept giving way, making me almost collapse on the stairs. Lorien would have to pull my knees back towards her to keep my legs straight. But laughed, and laughed, and laughed.

Having any form of disability, whether it is visible or not, can be debilitating. Your frame of mind can affect the responses of those around you. I make fun of my disability, and I invite others to do the same. Making people laugh and laughing with them makes me feel normal and stops people from thinking that they must treat me differently or give me special treatment.

Now is the part that I was not looking forward to: Karin having to get me undressed, put my pyjamas on me and get me into bed. I had to instruct her on the best way to do it to minimise the pain. I still didn't have entire movement in my arm on the side of my operation (and even now, over a year post-op, it hasn't returned to normal; it quite probably never will at this stage, but I've found workarounds), so I was unable to lift my arm above my head to remove my top. Karin carefully worked out the best way to do this. The last garment that needed to be removed was always my socks, which help protect my feet when my trousers are taken off. But to remove my socks, she had to be really quick, like the ripping of a band-aid. I would still scream or grunt in pain, as even this slight movement was sheer agony. It would cause the sensation of razor blades being embedded into my skin and then being dragged up my legs. I still had to wear the surgical bra, which has to be worn 24 hours a day for 6 - 8 weeks after your operation, so this stayed on. I showed her my boob anyway because, you know, why not? I think sometimes people are curious but don't know how to ask.

Once I was ready for bed, Karin tucked me in, made sure I was comfortable, and then went to the next room to check in with Lorien quickly. I must have fallen asleep immediately, as I don't recall Karin coming to bed.

The following day, the sound of Karin's laughter woke me up. Opening my eyes, I see that she is standing over me in fits of laughter. Apparently, I took a while to come around, and she had been taking the mick out of me again. She regaled me of what I had been saying in response to her, and it made me laugh after realising that she was indeed telling the truth.

After breakfast, we met with the Hotel Manager, Dorita. We explained our findings and came up with a plan for making the hiring of parts of the hotel profitable in quieter times.

Travelling home, I was feeling so tired that I managed to stay awake for about half an hour. I only woke up when I heard Karin's laughter again. She had pulled into a lay-by to take a photo of me sleeping. Apparently, I was pouting. As far as I know, I do not pout when conscious, but it seems I more than make up for it when I am asleep.

4th June 2023 - We are back at the Talbot Hotel to meet with Dorita, Lorien, Richard Felix and his wife Julia. Discussions on Richard orating one of his excellent haunted history talks took place. At the end of the meeting, date, the number of tickets and the costs were agreed upon.

Richard and Julia were very kind in helping me navigate the hotel during our mini-investigation. They never talked down to me or made me feel disabled. Julia told me to slow down and that I needed to learn to walk before I could run. She also told me that she could tell that I was stubborn and that she would need to keep an eye on me.

SEEING OLD FRIENDS AGAIN

15th July 2023 - Some of my paranormal friends were attending an investigation at Nothe Fort in Weymouth, which Rachel Hayward had organised. I have investigated here once before and it is an intriguing building.

I secretly messaged her, asking if I could pop in for a cuppa to see everyone, as I was missing them all immensely. Simon had agreed to drive me there if I felt up to it. I hadn't realised how far it was from us, but it took nearly an hour and a half to get there.

Pulling into the large courtyard of the Fort, I could see all of my friends in the base room. When they spotted me getting out of the car, with Simons's assistance as he moved my wheels in front of me, there were exclamations of 'It's Lisa!'

Rachel had robbed her husband's spirits cupboard and gave Simon a bottle of his Welsh Whiskey; he loved it, so it didn't last long. She also gave me a beautiful bunch of flowers.

I could have cried as each of them wrapped their arms around me, telling me how well I looked; I knew they were lying because, as far as I was concerned, I looked like death. But it was wonderful to see them all.

Sarah took Simon for a quick tour of the Fort whilst I chatted with everyone.

David told me that the lift wasn't working, but they would all help me get around if need be. He thought that I had come to investigate. While I would have loved to have stayed with them and joined them for the evening, I knew that my energy levels wouldn't allow it.

Driving home, Simon said that he now understood why I loved investigating the paranormal. Not only do we get access to some of the United Kingdom's best heritage locations, but I also have wonderful friends. Meeting some of them helped him worry less when I went away.

I have embraced returning to the paranormal field and have attended a few investigations now. The ones that stand out the most are these.

BACK AT THE JAMAICA INN

September 2023
This was a busy month for me and the paranormal
My first paranormal event back at the Jamaica Inn was a breeze. The staff were amazing, and I was so pleased to see them all. Kate, the manager, had put measures in place to ensure that I felt safe and was able to help run the event with the rest of the team.

Because of the severe fatigue that I now suffer from, after we arrived at the Inn and I had said my hellos to everyone, I went back to our room to sleep. Sometime later, Karin came and woke me; it was time to make our way to the restaurant, ready to greet our guests before dinner. After we had all finished our meal, Karin, Rachael and I introduced ourselves and explained how the evening would run and where to assemble if the fire alarm sounded. Karin made a joke, saying to leave me behind as I'll take too long to get to safety.

There are two entry points to the lower restaurant where we were gathered, there are some steps, and then at the other end of the restaurant, there is a ramp. Rachael took half of the guests upstairs to investigate the haunted bedrooms, whilst Karin and I were going to take our guests to the museum and stable block. Karin told the guests to meet us at the top of the stairs as we were going to go via the ramp. The guests were nowhere in sight when we got to the top of the stairs. We looked behind us and saw an orderly line of guests following behind us. We all laughed when Karin pointed at the stairs and said that she meant for them to come that way.

The evening went well, and the guests all had a fantastic time.

The Old Vicarage Hotel in Bridgewater. Karin and I decided to stay in Room 5, which was the largest, so it could be used as the base room until the restaurant and bar closed. Room 5 is up one flight of stairs and haunted, so everyone who attended wanted to investigate it. Staying in this room meant I couldn't go to bed until after 1.30 am or thereabouts. At this point, my body had had enough, and all of the symptoms from my neuropathy had increased significantly. Steve practically carried me up the stairs; I do not know how he managed it. With everything hurting like hell, all I could do was let this happen without offering any assistance with the task. I couldn't bear touching anything, so my hands were limp like wet lettuces; it reminded me of the 'Flower Pot Men', so I just kept saying 'flubalubalub' to the laughter of the group of friends who were getting me up the stairs.

Karin and Kim sat me on the toilet, undressed me, and dressed me in my nightwear. I was unable to get off the toilet, so Steve was called in to assist. He then did a sort of 'tuck and roll' manoeuvre to get me into bed. I slept as if I were dead. When it was time to wake up the following morning, I struggled to rise. Karin helped me sit up and then proceeded to dress me in my day clothes while I was half asleep.

January 2024 - We are again at the Jamaica Inn, this time for a private investigation with some friends. I always have a nanna-nap in the afternoon, and Karin or another team member will come and wake me up when it is time to start the evening.

This time, Karin was tasked with waking me. I woke up quite quickly, which is unusual for me. Karin was getting herself ready, brushing her hair, etc. So I thought that rather than wait for her to help me out of bed, I would do it myself. I could see my wheels at the bottom of the bed, and in my head, this would work. If I were to roll down the bed, I could hold onto my wheels and stand up. It didn't!

I rolled down the bed and ended up face down at the end of it, desperately grasping the duvet as I gradually sank to the floor onto my knees, screaming, 'It didn't work, it didn't work'.

Karin was a great help - she stood there laughing, then took photos of my face and then my arse. She tried to lift me but wasn't able to as I was a dead weight. Through tears of laughter, she phoned Steve and told him that I had fallen off the bed and she couldn't get me up.

Christ knows what he must have thought, but we heard him running down the corridor towards our room to assist me.

Seeing me leant over the bed on my knees, he proceeded to dry-hump me before lifting me to my feet. I honestly can't remember laughing so much at this.

February 2024 - Jamaica Inn. Karin and I were going to take some new photos and film some video content for media and marketing. We also planned to go Live on FaceBook to introduce the team members and answer some of the questions that members of the public had asked. We have brought Kev and Lorien with us this time. Lorien is a fantastic author; her words can transport you back in time so you can live the events through someone else's eyes. Kevin Charity had tasked her to write a spooky book for each of the Hotels owned by Coaching Inn Group. Unfortunately, this didn't come to fruition after a change of management. Kev is a technology expert, so we asked if he could assist us. His help and advice on what would work best was invaluable.

We had arranged to visit Richard at the nearby Pengenna Manor to discuss an upcoming event. Travelling down narrow country roads had never bothered me previously; in fact, I learned to drive on them, but the way my brain was operating at the moment, my repeated phrase was 'I hate my brain', and the journey was frightening for me. I tried my best to keep my fears under control, but when we came face to face with a swollen Forde, I could feel my grasp on them weakening.

It was decided between Kev and Karin to 'floor it'. Water came up over the bonnet and the front windshield. Seeing the water cover the car, I could feel the last threads of my control snapping. Encountering a small car coming the other way, Karin stopped and automatically moved to put the car in reverse.

The fear I felt made my words sound venomous, 'don't you dare go back'. In my mind, we were on a cliff edge; if she were to go back, we could fall off and all die.

The poor couple we were forced to reverse might well now be divorced. The woman who was driving hit every single corner of the car on the banks. The male, who I assume was her husband, tried to give her advice, to which she ripped his head off. If this couple ever read this book, I would like to apologise for the ensuing argument that I caused.

Once she reversed into a passing area, we drove past her and continued on to the Manor, which was just around the corner.

When we arrived at the Manor, I began to relax and calm down. It is a fantastic property, so tranquil and surrounded by Cornish hills.

I wasn't looking forward to the journey back to the Inn, and I hoped that we wouldn't have to go through the Forde again. Luckily, we didn't; we went across Bodmin Moor, which was one hundred times worse.

The road was incredibly windy, and each time it disappeared, either around a sharp corner or over the brow of a hill, I thought the road had disappeared, and we would all fall to our deaths. I didn't have time to calm down from one incident to the next, and I quickly became hysterical. In all the years that I have known Karin, she has never known what I am afraid of. Slowing down, she pointed out a horse on my side of the car.

'Ah, look at the little horse.'

Bear in mind that I am already hysterical; my grasp on reality has gone. I screamed, 'I'm scared of horses' whilst punching

Karin in the arm, trying to make her drive whilst also trying to climb over the sizeable centre console at the same time.

Everyone, bar me, was in fits of laughter.

All I could do was 'brace' as each scary thing happened. I'm not sure who started it, but eventually they all joined in shouting 'Look out', 'What's that?', or Karin would brake hard. Each time, I got more and more scared.

There was a concrete bridge over a perfectly calm pond. The sky and surrounding fauna echoed on its surface. It was probably a couple of inches deep. But in my head, it was a raging torrent of water. The bridge was rickety and crumbling, and we were all going to die. They all decided to stop on this bridge. I was beside myself with fear, my heart beating so erratically that I swear it was about to stop.

Of course, looking back, we laugh about it. At the time, I tried to laugh, too. I knew that my friends wouldn't put me in danger and that what they said was the truth, but my mind would not allow me to sway from the course it had decided to take me down.

March 2024 - Karin was invited to talk at Scary South West, a conference for the paranormal. She was allowed a plus one, and she invited me, which was lovely of her. The conference was taking place in Bude, Devon. We were booked to stay in a local hotel for two nights, and some of our friends would also be there: Kev, Lorien, Rachel, Kim, Sabrina, Kate, Amy and Jayne; if I have forgotten anyone, please forgive me. On Friday night, I found a local restaurant that could accommodate us all at short notice. From the map, it looked as if it were a short walk over the bridge; I had progressed from my rollator to crutches, but as I had only had them for a couple of days, I was still getting to grips with how to use them. Believe it or not, it is harder than it looks.

After our meal, we headed back to the hotel. I was, at this point, completely exhausted. Trying to get back to the hotel with no energy whatsoever was extremely difficult. With the help of my friends, I managed it. Their help consisted of taking the mick out of me, making me think that they were going to make me run back to the hotel. Through laughter, we got there.

April 2024 - We rented a haunted cottage in the Welsh hills and are away for two nights. Admittedly, the accessibility wasn't great for me, but with the help of my friends, I managed to get around the whole building. Simon dropped me off at Karin's on Friday morning; after a cup of tea and a quick check that we had everything, we made our way to collect Rachel. We arrived on Friday afternoon, a little later than we were expecting. This was purely my fault; I found everything on the Journey frightening and would wave my hands around while making panicked noises. If Karin drove more than 30 miles an hour, I would begin to flap; the country roads were even worse, and I made her crawl around the corners at a snail's pace.

It was soon realised that my condition was getting worse and was affecting every aspect of my life. Especially after Karin put her stationery car into reverse, which made it jolt, I instinctively grabbed the steering wheel. I have no recollection of this, but I have it on good authority that this did actually happen. So not only was I becoming a nervous wreck, but my condition was also becoming dangerous.

After we had returned from our meal out on Saturday night, Sarah, Rachel, and I decided to sit at the dining table and use the Quija Board. The table was old and very long, with a bench that was just as long on either side of it. I tried to pull the bench out slightly so that I could get in, but it was so heavy that I wasn't able to shift it. In my head, this would work; I sat on the bench with my back to the table and tried to swing my legs around. What happened next was another comedic moment; in slow motion, I began slipping off of the bench. When I finally stopped moving, I found myself wedged between the table and the bench. The only thing that was stopping me from falling into a heap on the floor was my boob. As my legs were so weak, I wasn't able to extricate myself from my position. Shouts were made that 'Lisa is stuck', and then Kev came to my rescue and helped me get out of my predicament; I was given strict instructions not to do that again. Trust me, there was no fear of that. It's quite embarrassing when you have to rely so heavily on people.

When I entered the Kitchen on Sunday morning, although I didn't notice it, everyone left one by one until it was just Kev and me in there. The conversation started like an everyday conversation, and then Kev began mentioning that he felt my condition was getting a lot worse, and it was becoming all-consuming. He asked me to visit the doctors and tell them that he believes that I am suffering from anxiety.

GEMMA TREDWIN

For Lisa

I know Lisa from working together as a small team of paranormal investigators, hosting events at the famous Jamaica Inn. She is excellent to work with, knowledgeable, fun, professional & often brutally honest, which I find hilarious & refreshing!

When I first learnt about Lisa's cancer diagnosis, I was shocked & upset. It hit me like a brick. Cancer can mean death, suffering & shitty uncertain times. Cancer killed my father back in 2020 & things were still raw. Karin, our team lead & wonderful friend, told me about Lisa's diagnosis & I knew I needed to be mindful of how Karin was also taking the news, as they are so close, the pair of them. I knew she would be strong for Lisa & go about things with humour, but deep down, I knew Karin would be frightened & concerned. I would message Lisa occasionally as I felt I didn't want to intrude or upset, but I thought of her often. I also feel guilty that I wasn't messaging enough. I would be updated by Karin at least weekly & would be an ear for Karin to share how she was feeling, get upset if she needed to & tell me how Lisa was doing.

We all remained hopeful & optimistic that Lisa would return to work with our lovely team at Jamaica Inn in October. We knew Lisa was determined & with her strong, resilient character, I hoped this would come true. After many, many arduous months of treatment & care, it did!

Lisa returned to work with us that October, as she had aimed for; I was so proud of her!

I hadn't seen her in all that time & was worried about saying or doing the wrong thing, but Lisa was & still is Lisa. She looked a bit different & her mobility, I could see, was a frustration for her & meant she couldn't climb the stairs to the "haunted bedrooms", but I had no doubt she would get up there one day when she & her body were strong enough. So, as a team, we would try &

make things work, supporting her to move with a walker about the old inn, helping her to bed early, dressing, getting her meds, etc. Often done with a warped sense of humour! I felt privileged that Lisa felt happy & trusted me with anything she needed help with during those times. At each event, I could see that she was getting stronger. Lisa walked upstairs at our last event in June 2024 this year. She is truly awesome!

Lisa is still brutally honest, so don't ask her for a new torch if you lose yours, as you'll get "the look." So hold on to your torches & don't anger her as she's still the same Lisa we know & love.

Gem Tredwin x

MY FINAL HOSPITAL ADMISSION - I HOPE

6th April 2024
And I'm in the hospital again. I joke that it is my favourite 5-star hotel. It isn't, but it helps you through. I have been admitted to the MAU and have a private side room. Apparently, this is the room that I was initially admitted to on Christmas Day. I have no recollection of it, though.

I'm cannulated, blood is taken, and then eventually, antibiotics are hooked up. Stool and urine samples are taken as and when I manage to produce them. I am no longer embarrassed by any of this. I suppose I have become numb to it now.

Simon leaves to go home, still having Harrison to sort out. Our poor boy has been an absolute trooper through everything.

Remembering how early the day starts in the hospital and that they have to keep the lights on throughout the night, albeit slightly dimmed, I was sensible and packed my sleep mask and earbuds. Let me reassure you that there is nothing kinky involved in these items. I need them when I go to the Jamaica Inn as I always need to have an afternoon's sleep. The hotel can be quite noisy, so these help make sure that I get some sleep.

After donning the mask and putting in the earbuds, I also remembered my pillow, and I settled down to sleep. I was only woken when they needed to swap out the antibiotics, hook up a saline solution, or take my observations, so I actually slept incredibly well.

Opting for toast for breakfast, I tuck in. Unable to finish it all, despite only two slices of bread, it's surprising how little you eat when in hospital. I don't know if it's because you are out of your comfort zone or if it's because you are worried about what the tests will reveal.

Simon's back, no doubt, came via the restaurant so that he

could indulge in a cooked breakfast. He confirms that he did, which makes me chuckle. We sat talking for a while about our plans for the future, and we always knew that I wanted to go down the writing route, not because I thought I would earn a living from it, but simply because I enjoy it. We never decide on a firm plan for Simon. He has been head- hunted by human resource companies, and whilst he doesn't relish the idea of returning to the corporate world of employment, we know that unless we get some plans in place soon, he will have no choice.

We have made many plans for how to earn an income once I can be left. He still wants to try bee-keeping and watchmaking. He has everything he needs, so there wouldn't need to be any financial outlay. It would just be a case of deciding on business names, registering them and building a website, there are obviously lots of other things involved in starting a business, and anyone who has gone down this route knows that you tick one thing off the list and then you think of something else, so the list never really seems to get any smaller.

He also wants to continue with the blind and shutters portion of my previous business. I explained that I have no problem building the website and doing the admin in the background, but that is as far as my involvement will be. You may think I am being unsupportive or selfish, but from my perspective, it caused a lot of pain and heartache to let the business go. I was proud of it; I watched it grow, and I nurtured it, so in a way, it was like a child. Also, visiting clients in their homes, helping them choose their window decor and not being able to do what I used to would be too much. It would bring to the forefront how much I had lost. So, if Simon wants to do this, I will do everything I can to support him and help it grow, similar to his bee-keeping and watchmaking businesses which he also has plans to begin.

So we have a plan; let's just hope that we can pull it off and earn a living from it. I don't think my dream of being a best-selling author is anywhere near a pipeline, let alone in it.

QUALITY OVER QUANTITY

10th April 2024

Since stopping the medication I feel so much better. The neuropathy pain in my hands and feet, although not completely gone, has diminished slightly. The brain fog and confusion have also lessened. I am not as tired either, and I haven't had to spend at least one day a week in bed. Again, this isn't like me. I am used to being on the go constantly from the second I get out of bed in the morning. I am also used to staying up until two or three in the morning due to the paranormal things that I frequently do, but since initially starting the medication, I would need to be in bed before eight.

I tell my oncologist that whilst things have settled down, they haven't returned to normal. He suggested that I make a doctor's appointment to get checked over and that he would call me in two weeks.

He asked if I was happy with this plan, and he has always been very accommodating. I informed him that I was giving serious consideration to not restarting this part of my treatment, and I explained to him the reasoning behind it.

To my surprise, he agreed that considering the amount of severe side effects that I have endured, possibly this treatment wasn't the right one for me. I explained that I am happy to stay on the endocrine part of the treatment because apart from the occasion hot flush (which is being controlled by a pill in the morning and one in the evening), I haven't experienced mood swings or the compulsion to kill my husband and bury him under the patio.

Simon asked him what the prognosis would be for stopping the treatment. He reassured us that up until three years ago, this drug wasn't in circulation; women with my type of cancer would only have endocrine treatment, and that was sufficient. He mentioned that he would like to see me in four weeks to check how I am and whether I had changed my mind, just in case. If I chose not to continue with the treatment, they would monitor me more closely and see me every three months.

Stopping treatment isn't for everyone I know, but for me, it is a decision that took a very long time to make. I would have needed to keep taking these pills for another sixteen months. I do not feel that I have any quality of life; barely being able to get up much before 11 am, having to spend an entire day in bed once a week, unable to complete even the most menial of tasks, living in constant pain, I could go on, but I don't want to bore you.

22nd May 2024
All of my appointments since being on the Abemacyclib medication have been over the phone, so being asked for a face-to-face meeting filled me with dread. I honestly thought that it would be a two-pronged attack, with them trying to persuade me to restart the medication.

I am so pleased that I was wrong in this instance. I met with the oncologist I always spoke with on the phone, so after so long, it was nice to put a face to the voice.

I tell him that I haven't changed my mind about the medication, and he agrees with me. He reiterates that I will be monitored more closely and seen in the clinic every three months.

He asked why I was using crutches, assuming that I must have hurt myself somehow. He looked shocked when I told him that it was the aftereffects of Chemotherapy and that I was still struggling on a daily basis. Simon told him everything he still has to do for me as I cannot.

He was surprised at the level of toxicity, so we asked how common this sort of thing is. Apparently, he had only seen two cases similar to mine during his entire career.

I told him that I had mentioned after my third infusion the

symptoms that I was experiencing, which were poo-pooed, and I was told that the treatment I had received so far wouldn't cause them.

He checked my notes, and I am assuming from his response that there is no mention of my symptoms or that the treatment had left me disabled, unable to walk unaided or care for myself completely. He said he would request a formal review of my case with his colleagues and superiors. Hopefully, this will enable them to put procedures in place so that another patient doesn't experience the failings that I have.

CLINTON BAPTISTE

5th May 2024 - Clinton Baptiste

We're here. I cannot believe that due to my diagnosis and having to cancel in 2022, we have finally made it, and we have front-row tickets to boot!

On the journey over, we are both yawning like you wouldn't believe; we are both tired and, unlike us, barely speak. Karin is lost in thought, no doubt feeling guilty for being out again instead of being at home trying to conquer the mountains of tasks that she has to do. I am quietly trying not to let the anxiety of being around lots of strangers invade my life. I am determined to stop allowing it to stop me from doing things I have missed out on so much, one because of my treatment and two because of the bloomin' anxiety!

The doors are opening, and we are going in! Because of my mobility issues (I am now on crutches), they let me in first. They probably saw me already nearly taking out one of the audience members when my crutch fell on him; it was so embarrassing!

We settled in the front row with the 'Paranormal Investigators on Tour 2024' sign I had made for the event. Karin propped my crutches up in the corner near the stage; I'm so anxious about inconveniencing people that I go out of my way to ensure that none of the apparel I need will interfere with anyone.

The warm-up act, 'comedy_mike' (he's on Instagram; check him out), was brilliant. He interacted with the audience and had us all laughing in no time.

Karin has a habit of talking to complete strangers, and the subject content is usually inappropriate. For instance, we had a paranormal business meeting in Bridgewater, and unbeknownst to me, you could make out the leopard print pattern on my knickers through my dress. As you can imagine, she relished in this and took every opportunity to let passers-by know this fact, to the point that one poor chap peddling on a bicycle nearly crashed into the church! I am constantly telling her to 'put the people down. The halfway drunken man behind us mentioned Bristol; how she heard this, I have no clue; she must have the hearing of a bat, but her ears picked up, and she couldn't help but engage in conversation with this poor man. I kept poking her, but she has clearly gotten used to this, as she completely ignored me.

Luckily, the intermission between 'comedy_mike' and 'Clinton Baptiste' wasn't that long, although I'm sure the chap Karin was speaking with thought it spread out into eternity.

The music begins, but I'm unsure of the soundtrack - I was too busy laughing. Standing on stage dressed in an oversized white silk gown, holding what looks like a broomstick that has been sawn in half in each hand, with the gown draped unceremoniously over them. He does a little 'sashaying' dance to the raucous laughter of some of the audience.

Then, I would like to say that in a well-rehearsed move, the gown was whipped off to reveal a sequin-encrusted three-piece suit. He must have been bloody hot under those lights in that get-up.

He begins with his very well-known phrase of 'aright. '

For those of you who have never seen or heard of Clinton Baptiste, if you like sarcastic humour and heckling (from the act, not the audience), then you will love him. His character plays a fake psychic medium with many powers and gifts of clairvoyance, half of which are probably made up.

For instance, at the end of the night, he breaks open fortune cookies, and he tells one gent that he predicts that 'his evening will end making love to a number of virgins'. As you can imagine, the audience either laughs or whoops. Clinton murmurs in his next breath, 'Where are we? Frome? Sorry I think you're out of luck there.'

Because Clinton clocked our Paranormal Tour sign, he picked on us the entire evening, even spraying us with a water pistol, calling Karin a dragon and me a carpet muncher. It was absolutely hilarious!

I was completely overwhelmed when he said that he had a special message for someone in the audience and pointed at me. Pre-cancer, I would never have gotten up on the stage; I would have told him to pick someone else. Mind you, pre-cancer, I would never have been sat in the front row holding a sign that is clearly inviting a comedian to rip into you.

Karin, in her excitement, started nudging me and saying, 'Go on then' She had completely forgotten that I'd need my crutches, which I couldn't reach. When he saw that I was on crutches, I can't recall exactly what he said, but I think it was along the lines of 'you're joking/bloody hell' on my way to the stage, he had me in fits with 'come on, hurry up, you slow bitch' 'what time do we have to be out of here tonight?' He waved his hands around, telling me, 'I've healed you; throw them away; you don't need them' Then, as I was climbing the stairs, he said, 'If you fall, you're not getting compensation'.

But I made it; I'm on the stage! Sitting on the stall, he asks me where are you from? What do you do? Now, I do quite a lot; I'm a paranormal investigator, a paranormal adviser, part of the famous Jamaica Inn Paranormal Team, an administrative assistant for an accountant and an author of, at that time, erotic fiction. So I thought, out of everything that I do, what would throw him completely? Obviously, I went with Author of Erotic Fiction (sorry, Alex, I did kind of set you up)

Then, pointing to my crutches, he said, 'So er, what's the issue here then?' Later, he told me he thought I'd sprained an ankle or something tedious.

When I told him 'I had cancer', he could not hold back the 'fuckin hell' and the rubbing of his face trying to compose himself. I honestly felt for him, he has a set that he needs to try to stick to, and now he has to rip the piss out of someone recovering from treatment. I did wonder if he would say that he'd have to pick someone else or try to tone it down a little. He whispered to me, 'I'm so sorry' my 'don't be, go for it!' And I am so glad that he did; the audience members got told off for saying that I needed to visit a hair salon; no one did, but it was a great gag with him shouting, 'Who said that? poor woman's in remission!'

I honestly cannot remember the last time I laughed so much that my stomach hurt. It was the best evening ever, and I cannot wait to see him on his next tour.

After the show, people came up to me to say what a great sport I was and that they initially thought that I was plant, until Clinton's reaction to me having had cancer. Even when we were leaving, I was questioned by locals asking where I'd been treated and how I found the hospital staff.

A POEM BY LISA

Still ...
By Lisa Holman

You look in the mirror, and a stranger is staring back at you
    But you are still you

Your appearance has changed beyond recognition
    But you are still you

Your mouth is full of ulcers, rendering speech difficult
    But you are still you

Your legs are weak and refuse to carry you
    But you are still you

Your hands feel like there are millions of needles stabbing you, making
everyday tasks excruciating
    But you are still you

Your feet are numb, so you stumble frequently
    But you are still you

Cancer has robbed you of so much,
But you are still here, and you are still you

As I look in the mirror, I remind myself
    I am still me

MOVING ON WITH LIFE

FINDING MYSELF AGAIN

I could easily be all doom and gloom and wring my hands in despair whilst repeating, 'Why me?' but what good would that do?

Before diagnosis, I knew what clothes looked good and what colours and styles I liked. After treatment, I don't know anymore. I have spent a small fortune on new clothes, trying to find myself again. I have a wardrobe full of lovely clothes that I feel aren't me anymore. Should I sell them? Donate them to a charity shop? Or hold onto them in the hopes that I will find myself again?

It isn't just that when I look in the mirror, I don't recognise myself anymore; I am also unable to do what I did previously. In some respects, it feels as if my life has ground to a halt.

The evening walks into town have stopped.
The four weekly runs as I trained for the Bath half have stopped.
The gym sessions, putting 25kg on my shoulders, squatting to the floor so my arse was a few inches away and then standing again, stopped.
Being able to help my friends has stopped.
Being able to cook a meal has stopped.
Getting into the bath has stopped.
Being independent has stopped.

Cancer has changed my life to the point that I don't recognise it any more. But rather than dwell on what I have lost, I am embracing what I have gained:
Time with my husband and family,
A gorgeous grandson
Discovering who my true friends are.
And most importantly, a second chance at life.

I am so determined to continue fighting and find the new me; Rachael calls me 'Mum 2.0', making me laugh and cry simultaneously.

I want to recover my mobility so I can run around with Frankie when he is older. I want to do everything I did with him that I did with my own children. I want him to know who Simon and I are, I want to be present in his life.

I also can't wait to travel and tick all of the things off of my bucket list.
The Valley of the Kings, The Grand Canyon, The Niagara Falls, Singapore to see the blossoms, Australia and New Zealand, to name a few.
As well as lots and lots of family holidays to create lasting memories.

I HATE MY BRAIN!

My cognitive ability still hasn't returned to 100%. I still struggle with forming sentences and lose track of what I am saying mid-flow.

Because my brain isn't firing on all cylinders, I often cannot separate fact from fiction, or make sense of the world around me.

For instance, one day, I looked through the glass of our log burner, and it looked different. There was clearly something in there. I looked closely and, in a state of panic, started screaming for Simon: 'There are hedgehogs in the fire, Simon, Simon, there are baby hedgehogs in the fire!' I was beside myself with panic.

Simon came into the lounge, looked at my state of absolute panic, opened the glass door, and showed me that what I thought were hedgehogs were actually fir cones.

We laughed at how stupid my brain currently is. I hope it doesn't take too long to return to full power, as some of my friends are enjoying its current state far more than they should.

HAIRCUT

It may seem ridiculous that I book an appointment with a hairdresser after losing all my hair and watching it slowly grow back.

I dithered a lot before speaking with Rachael about what to do with my hair. My daughter is terrific; throughout my treatment, she researched different things to help with my symptoms and was no different regarding my hair.

She found a hairdresser in Bath that specialised in people who had gone through chemotherapy and lost their hair and how the treatment had changed the make-up of the follicles.

After everything I had been through, I was extremely nervous about going to a hairdresser, knowing they are usually packed with people. Rachael booked an appointment with Laura at The Suite in Bath, and she arranged to pick me up, telling me that she would stay with me throughout my appointment to give me moral support.

Meeting Laura instantly set me at ease. She explained that her mum had also had Breast Cancer some years ago. After washing and cutting my hair, she showed me how to blow dry it so it wasn't as curly or frizzy.

The staff are lovely and very amenable to my condition each time I visit. I now have the confidence to go to my appointments on my own. Simon enjoys window shopping in Bath whilst I am being pampered, and then we go to The Walcot restaurant a few doors down for a light bite.

SLIMMING WORLD

In another attempt to find myself again, I rejoined Slimming World with my friend Narva.

Stepping onto the scales the first time took a mammoth effort, but with Narvas and Claires (the consultant) help, I managed it.

Each week, I watched as my weight crept north instead of south, but I was still committed to trying to lose weight. At the time, I believed that I was 100% focused on the cause. But looking back I realise that I was just going through the motions.

I hadn't long come to the end of my treatment, my immunity was still dangerously low, the anxiety that every visit caused was debilitating. I told myself that I would not let my mental health win, and that I would continue to attend.

I was completely overwhelmed when I was nominated for 'Woman of the Year 2023'; I had to give a little speech, but after the first sentence, I couldn't continue, so Narva finished it for me. Listening to all of the nominees and the battles they had faced and overcome made me more determined to get on board and stick to the plan 100%.

I was training for the Bath Half Marathon at the beginning of last year. With a strict training regime, I had never felt better. Unfortunately, the marathon was cancelled last year and postponed to this year, so I could not participate.
In September, I was diagnosed with grade 4 breast cancer that had spread to my lymph nodes. I had 6 rounds of chemotherapy, which caused severe infections, and a few bouts of sepsis, which was great. I have now completed the main portion of my treatment, including surgery and radiotherapy.
The side effect of chemo has left me with mobility issues, and the weight has just continued to pile on; where I now lead a more sedentary lifestyle but continue to consume the food I did while in training.

And whilst I don't always see the results I wish on the scales, I continue to come to group and take ownership of the food I chose to eat through the week.

The new eating regime will eventually hold firm through the week, and I will see amazing weight loss. Especially as I have now found a way to start exercising again by joining the gym and swimming a couple of times already.

So, whilst my story doesn't necessarily focus on weight loss, it does focus on mind, body, and soul.

Check your breasts when you get home tonight and put a reminder in your calendar to do it every month, and for you men who are here, don't think you are immune as I met a lovely chap who was being treated for breast cancer at the same time as me.

Everyone at the club then voted for who they thought was the most deserving of this award; I couldn't believe it when Claire called my name. After all, I was a relatively new member, and my story wasn't about weight loss, and I hadn't actually lost anything, which is the sole purpose of this group.

After winning this award I became more determined than ever. Unfortunately, fate had other ideas and threw Clostridium difficile colitis into the works. Trying to recover from another infection, which had been caused by the sheer amount of antibiotics that needed to be taken to fight previous infections, destroyed the small amount of mental health that I had recovered.

I stopped attending group, I stopped watching what I ate, telling myself each time that I had been through hell, so I deserved to eat whatever the f**k I wanted!

I'm sure that you can guess what happened next. The weight piled on. My mental health became worse and I hit rock bottom. I never allowed anyone to see how much I was struggling for fear of alienating them. I put on a happy face every single time.

After stopping the anti-cancer medication, my mental health

began to improve. I began to feel more like me. Yes, I still suffer from awful anxiety, and I suspect a large amount of PTSD, but under the surface, I can feel myself returning.

I have rejoined Slimming World, I attend on my own, I drive myself there, and Claire helps me get on the scales. Some weeks I lose, some weeks I put on, but I have lost a grand total of two pounds, and I couldn't be happier. I know that with everything else it will be a long battle, but I will get there, and I will eventually find myself again!

WHAT YOU CAN DO

Challenge everything - ask questions
DO NOT google anything relating to your cancer!
Don't forget to take things to occupy yourself when going to appointments
Always take an overnight bag in the car
Never pass up the opportunity to have a drink
Don't assume that your symptoms are normal, ask for help

Things that may help Skin
Udderly cream from Amazon - your skin dries out, so moisturising regularly is important; your feet may crack and bleed.
Dry Scalp Treatment from the Beauty Despite Cancer website - your scalp will love you for this. Apply it at bedtime, and the scent of lavender will help you sleep.

Mouth
Biotene mouthwash and toothpaste - your mouth will feel like the Sahara Desert whilst licking Ghandis flip-flops.
A soft toothbrush or even one for babies - your gums may hurt and bleed
Frozen pineapple - be careful not to eat too much of this as it can cause mouth ulcers

Nails
Cuticle oil
Hand cream - a good quality one.

Sleep
Pillow-mist
Lavender Oil

Hair
When my hair began growing back, I invested in an Intense Thickening shampoo from Grow Gorgeous. It isn't cheap, but I have found that it has made my hair grow quicker than it ever

has, and it is also thicker. So it is well worth the investment.

Websites that can offer support

Look Good Feel Better - they run workshops from yoga to how to use make-up to look like eyebrows

Macmillan - they offer support and guidance to cancer patients and can point you in the right direction for financial assistance.

Breast Cancer Now - again, they offer support for patients

Depending on your type of cancer, there are various cancer charities and websites. A quick Google search will point you in the right direction.

What you can do to support your friend(s)
The most important thing is to keep in touch. Message them, saying that you don't expect them to respond immediately, but you are thinking of them.

If you can afford it, buy them a little gift. Something they can use to pamper themselves, like a nice-smelling candle or bath bombs, it doesn't need to be expensive. Or you could get them something really nice by putting together a group of friends.

If you are a baker, make some little cupcakes and take them around.

If you can make a nice soup, they will really appreciate it.

If you know that they and their families are struggling to make healthy meals, make something that can be heated up.

When you are going shopping, message them and ask them if there is anything that they need.

Send a 'thinking of you' card occasionally.

Patients going through chemotherapy shouldn't have plants or cut flowers near them; these can cause infections. But if you are crafty, you could make some paper ones. There are lots of tutorials on YouTube for how to make them.

Send them something that will keep them occupied, a colouring book, diamond art or something similar.

Ask if they'd like to go for a walk with you or even for a drive-through coffee.

If you have time on your hands, you could offer to take them to their appointments.

When they are going through radiotherapy, it can be quite draining for the person who takes them every day; perhaps you could offer to help with this.

Arrange a virtual get-together with a group of friends, where you can chat about what has been happening in your lives.

But I cannot stress enough how important it is that you stay in contact with them, even if they don't message you back. Trust me, the fact that you have thought of them will mean a lot to them.

IN THE END

I have tried my damnedest to not allow the cancer, and the problems that I experienced throughout my treatment, or the results thereof, to change me. I have found that humour, rudeness, and inappropriateness have helped to get me through.

From Karin whistling at me, tapping her legs and shouting 'here boy' whilst I am pushing my rollator trying desperately to keep up with her, too stubborn (or scared) to let her push me, the constant Andy and Lou sketches from Little Britain, and then being called 'Lezzy Lisa' when my hair began to grow back. It all helped to get me through it.

I hope that you have found my mumblings useful, whether you are or have been a cancer patient, or if you know someone that is currently battling this horrendous disease. Most of all I hope that if you know someone who is currently being affected by cancer, that my writing has helped you understand what they may be thinking and feeling. If this book helps a single person to feel as if they haven't suddenly become invisible to the people who should love and care about them, then I feel as if I have achieved my goal. And I hope that you managed to laugh along with me.

What I would like you to take from this is that no topic should be a taboo, if we do not talk about things freely how on earth are we expected to learn and grow?

Take care of those in your life that you love. Remember today is a gift and tomorrow isn't promised.

Much love Lisa xx

MEDICAL EXPLANATIONS

In this section, you will find the Medical explanations in detail. This information was compiled through using online searches and ChatGPT.

I hope that you find this useful and that it gives you an insight into how poorly you can sometimes become.

ABEMACYCLIB

Abemacyclib (brand name Verzenio) is a medication used in the treatment of certain types of breast cancer. As a targeted therapy, it works by inhibiting cyclin-dependent kinases 4 and 6 (CDK4/6), which are proteins that play a key role in cell division and cancer growth. While effective, Abemacyclib can cause a range of side effects, some of which can be serious. Here's a detailed overview of the common, less common, and serious side effects associated with Abemacyclib:

Common Side Effects - I developed 1 - 2 - 3 - 5 - 6

1. Diarrhoea - The most common side effect, often occurring within the first few days of treatment. It can usually be managed with antidiarrheal medications and by maintaining hydration.

2. Fatigue - Patients may experience tiredness and a general lack of energy.

3. Nausea - Often mild to moderate, nausea can sometimes be managed with dietary adjustments and anti-nausea medications.

4. Vomiting - Can occur, though it is less common than nausea.

5. Abdominal Pain - Some patients report stomach pain or discomfort.

6. Decreased Appetite - This can lead to weight loss in some individuals.

7. Infection - Increased risk of infections due to reduced white blood cell counts.

8. Anaemia - Lowered red blood cell count leading to symptoms like fatigue and shortness of breath.

9. Thrombocytopenia - Reduced platelet count, which can increase the risk of bleeding and bruising.

Less Common Side Effects I developed 3 - 6

1. Mouth Sores (Stomatitis) - Painful sores or ulcers in the mouth.

2. Rash - Skin rashes or other skin-related issues.

3. **Hair Thinning or Loss** - Some patients may experience changes in hair density.

4. **Elevated Liver Enzymes** - Indicating potential liver stress or damage, usually monitored through blood tests.

5. **Kidney Function Changes** - Possible alterations in kidney function, also monitored through blood tests.

6. **Dry Mouth** - Reduced saliva production leading to discomfort.

Serious Side Effects I developed 1 - 2

1. **Severe Diarrhoea** - Leading to dehydration and electrolyte imbalance, requiring medical intervention.

2. **Severe Infection** - Due to neutropenia (a significant reduction in neutrophils, a type of white blood cell), increasing the risk of serious infections like sepsis.

3. **Pulmonary Embolism** - A blood clot in the lungs, presenting with symptoms like sudden shortness of breath, chest pain, and rapid heart rate.

4. **Deep Vein Thrombosis (DVT)** - Blood clots in the legs, which can cause swelling, pain, and redness.

5. **Severe Anaemia** - Requiring blood transfusions or other medical interventions.

6. **Severe Liver Injury** - Rare but serious, potentially leading to liver failure.

Management of Side Effects

Diarrhoea - Managed with anti-diarrhoea medications (e.g., loperamide), hydration, and dietary adjustments.

Fatigue - Regular light exercise, adequate rest, and maintaining a balanced diet can help manage fatigue.

Nausea/Vomiting - Anti-nausea medications and dietary changes can provide relief.

Infection Prevention - Good hygiene, avoiding crowds, and prompt treatment of infections can mitigate risks.

Monitoring - Regular blood tests to monitor blood counts and liver and kidney function are crucial for the early detection and management of side effects.

Precautions
Regular Monitoring - Frequent blood tests to monitor for potential side effects.

Immediate Reporting - Patients should immediately report any signs of infection, severe diarrhoea, or unusual symptoms to their healthcare provider.

Medication Interactions - Abemacyclib can interact with other medications, so it's important to discuss all medications and supplements being taken with the healthcare provider.

Conclusion
While Abemacyclib is an effective treatment for certain types of breast cancer, it comes with a range of potential side effects. Careful monitoring and proactive management of these side effects are essential to ensure the best possible outcome and quality of life for patients undergoing treatment. Always consult with a healthcare provider for personalised advice and management strategies tailored to individual needs.

ACUPUNCTURE

Acupuncture is a traditional Chinese medical practice that involves inserting thin needles into specific points on the body to promote healing and improve overall well-being. This practice has been used for thousands of years and is based on the concept of balancing the body's energy, known as "Qi" or "chi." Here's a detailed explanation of acupuncture, including its principles, how it is performed, its uses, and potential benefits and risks:

Principles of Acupuncture
Qi and Meridians
Concept of Qi - In traditional Chinese medicine (TCM), Qi is the vital life force that flows through the body. It is believed that a balanced and uninterrupted flow of Qi is essential for health and well-being.

Meridians - Qi flows through pathways in the body called meridians. There are 12 primary meridians, each associated with specific organs and functions. Blockages or imbalances in the flow of Qi through these meridians are thought to cause illness and discomfort.

Accupoints
Definition - Specific points along the meridians where needles are inserted are called accupoints or acupuncture points. There are over 350 recognised accupoints on the human body.

Stimulation - By stimulating these accupoints, practitioners aim to restore the balance of qi and promote the body's natural healing processes.

How Acupuncture is Performed
Initial Consultation
Assessment - The acupuncturist begins with a comprehensive assessment of the patient's health history, symptoms, and lifestyle. This may include examining the tongue, checking the pulse, and asking about various aspects of health.

Diagnosis - Based on the assessment, the practitioner

determines the pattern of imbalance and selects the appropriate accupoints for treatment.

Procedure
Sterilisation - The acupuncturist uses sterile, single-use, thin needles.

Insertion - The needles are inserted into the skin at specific accupoints. The depth of insertion varies depending on the location and the desired effect, usually ranging from a few millimetres to a couple of centimetres.

Manipulation - The needles may be gently twisted, moved up and down, or left in place for a certain period, typically 15 to 30 minutes. Some practitioners use additional methods like electrical stimulation or heat (moxibustion) to enhance the effects.

Sessions - The number of sessions required depends on the condition being treated and the individual's response to therapy. Some conditions may improve after a few sessions, while others may require ongoing treatment.

Uses of Acupuncture
Acupuncture is used to address a wide range of conditions, including:

Pain Management
Chronic Pain - Conditions like lower back pain, neck pain, osteoarthritis, and migraines.

Acute Pain - Injuries, dental pain, and post-surgical pain.

Mental Health
Anxiety and Depression - Helping to alleviate symptoms and improve mood.

Stress - Reducing stress levels and promoting relaxation.

General Health
Digestive Issues - Conditions such as irritable bowel syndrome (IBS) and nausea (including chemotherapy-induced nausea).

Respiratory Issues - Allergies, asthma, and sinusitis.

Women's Health - Menstrual cramps, infertility, and menopausal symptoms.

Potential Benefits and Risks
Benefits
Holistic Approach - Acupuncture considers the whole person, aiming to restore balance and promote overall well-being.
Complementary Treatment - It can be used alongside conventional medical treatments to enhance their effectiveness and reduce side effects.
Minimal Side Effects - When performed by a qualified practitioner, acupuncture generally has few side effects.

Risks
Infection - Although rare, there is a risk of infection if non-sterile needles are used.
Bleeding and Bruising - Minor bleeding or bruising can occur at the needle insertion sites.
Discomfort - Some people may experience mild discomfort, dizziness, or soreness during or after the treatment.
Inappropriate for Some Conditions - Certain health conditions may not be suitable for acupuncture, and it's essential to consult with a healthcare provider before starting treatment.

Acupuncture is a widely recognised and respected component of traditional Chinese medicine that offers a holistic approach to health and wellness. By addressing the body's energy flow, acupuncture can provide relief for various conditions and enhance overall well-being, making it a valuable complementary therapy in modern healthcare.

BIOPSY

A breast biopsy is a medical procedure used to remove a small sample of breast tissue for laboratory testing to determine whether a breast lump or abnormality is benign (non-cancerous) or malignant (cancerous). Here's a detailed description of what is typically involved in a breast biopsy:

Pre-procedure Preparation
Consultation and Consent
A doctor will explain the procedure, its risks, and benefits.
The patient will sign a consent form.
Imaging Studies
Mammograms, ultrasounds, or MRIs may be used to locate the area of concern.
Types of Breast Biopsies
There are several types of breast biopsies, including:

Fine-Needle Aspiration (FNA)
Procedure
- A thin, hollow needle is inserted into the breast lump or abnormal area. Cells and fluid are aspirated (drawn out).
Advantages - Quick and minimally invasive.
Disadvantages - May not provide enough tissue for a definitive diagnosis.

Core Needle Biopsy
Procedure
- A larger, hollow needle is used to remove a small cylinder of tissue. Typically guided by imaging (ultrasound, mammogram, or MRI).
Advantages - Provides more tissue for analysis.
Disadvantages - More invasive than FNA but still minimally invasive.

Stereotactic Biopsy
Procedure
- The patient lies face down on a special table with the breast

positioned through an opening.

- Mammograms are taken from different angles to locate the exact area.

- A needle or vacuum-assisted device is used to remove tissue samples.

Advantages - Highly precise for abnormalities not palpable by touch.

Disadvantages - Requires specialised equipment and positioning.

Vacuum-Assisted Biopsy
Procedure

- A vacuum-powered instrument is inserted through a small incision.

- Multiple tissue samples can be taken through one needle insertion.

Advantages - More tissue can be removed than with a core needle biopsy.

Disadvantages - More invasive and may require a small incision.

Surgical (Open) Biopsy
Procedure

- A surgeon removes part or all of the lump through an incision in the breast.

Advantages - Provides the largest tissue sample.

Disadvantages - Most invasive, with longer recovery time and potential for scarring.

During the Procedure
Anaesthesia

- Local anaesthesia is typically used to numb the area.

- In some cases, especially with surgical biopsies, general anaesthesia may be used.

Positioning

- The patient is positioned depending on the type of biopsy (e.g., lying on back, side, or stomach).

Guidance

- Imaging techniques (ultrasound, mammogram, or MRI) may be used to guide the needle to the precise location.

Sample Collection

- Tissue samples are collected through the needle or via a small incision.
- Pressure is applied to the site to minimise bleeding.

Post-procedure Care
Wound Care

The biopsy site is covered with a sterile bandage.

Instructions on keeping the area clean and dry are provided.

Pain Management

Over-the-counter pain relievers (e.g., acetaminophen) may be recommended.

Activity Restrictions

Patients may be advised to avoid strenuous activities for a day or two.

Follow-up

The patient will receive instructions on when to expect results and schedule a follow-up appointment.

Laboratory Analysis

The tissue sample is sent to a pathology lab.

A pathologist examines the tissue under a microscope to check for abnormal or cancerous cells.

Results are typically available within a few days to a week.

Risks and Complications

Bleeding or Bruising - Some bleeding and bruising at the biopsy site are common.

Infection - Rare but possible; signs include increased redness, swelling, or drainage.

Pain - Some discomfort at the biopsy site, which is usually manageable with pain relievers.

Overall, a breast biopsy is a critical step in diagnosing breast conditions, allowing for appropriate and timely treatment planning.

BISPHOSPHONATES

Bisphosphonates are a class of drugs commonly prescribed to treat osteoporosis and other bone-related conditions. While effective, they can have several side effects, ranging from mild to severe. Here are the common side effects:

Common Side Effects
Gastrointestinal Issues:
1. Nausea
2. Abdominal pain
3. Dyspepsia (indigestion)
4. Constipation or diarrhoea
5. Oesophagitis (inflammation of the oesophagus)
6. Gastric ulcers

Musculoskeletal Pain:
1. Bone pain
2. Muscle pain
3. Joint pain

Flu-like Symptoms:
1. Fever
2. Fatigue
3. Malaise

Serious Side Effects
Oesophageal Irritation and Ulceration:
1. Esophagitis
2. Oesophageal ulcers
3. Potential risk of oesophageal cancer with long-term use

Osteonecrosis of the Jaw (ONJ):
1. A serious condition characterised by the death of bone tissue in the jaw, often associated with invasive dental procedures.

Atypical Femoral Fractures:
1. Unusual fractures of the thigh bone, typically with minimal or no trauma.

Renal Impairment:
1. Possible kidney damage or renal failure, especially in

patients with preexisting renal conditions.

Hypocalcemia:

1. Low levels of calcium in the blood, which can cause muscle spasms, cramps, or more severe symptoms.

Uveitis and Scleritis:

1. Inflammation of the uvea and sclera in the eyes, potentially causing pain and vision problems.

Rare Side Effects

Severe Allergic Reactions:

1. Anaphylaxis, although extremely rare.

Severe Skin Reactions:

1. Stevens - Johnson syndrome
2. Toxic epidermal necrolysis

Monitoring and Management

Dental Health: Regular dental check-ups and maintaining good oral hygiene can help reduce the risk of ONJ.

Calcium and Vitamin D: Supplementing with calcium and vitamin D may be necessary to prevent hypocalcemia.

Renal Function: Regular monitoring of kidney function is recommended, especially in patients with preexisting conditions.

Patients taking bisphosphonates should be aware of these potential side effects and discuss any concerns with their healthcare provider. Monitoring for symptoms and maintaining regular check-ups can help mitigate some of these risks.

CPR

Resuscitation after the heart stops, commonly known as cardiopulmonary resuscitation (CPR), is a critical emergency procedure aimed at maintaining blood flow and oxygenation to vital organs until professional medical help can arrive. Here's a detailed guide on how to perform CPR and the potential complications that can arise afterward.

How to Perform CPR

Assess the Situation
Ensure the scene is safe for both the rescuer and the victim.
Check for responsiveness by shaking the person gently and shouting their name.

Call for Help
If the person is unresponsive, call emergency services immediately or instruct someone else to do so.
If available, have someone get an automated external defibrillator (AED).

Open the Airway
Place the person on their back on a firm surface.
Tilt the head back slightly and lift the chin to open the airway.

Check for Breathing
Look for chest movement, listen for breathing sounds, and feel for breath on your cheek for no more than 10 seconds.
If there is no breathing or only gasping, proceed to CPR.

Perform Chest Compressions

Hand Placement - Place the heel of one hand on the centre of the chest (on the lower half of the sternum). Place your other hand on top and interlock your fingers.

Compression Technique - Keep your elbows straight and use your body weight to compress the chest at least 2 inches (5 cm) deep.

Rate - Aim for a rate of 100-120 compressions per minute.

Quality - Allow the chest to fully recoil between compressions.

Give Rescue Breaths
After 30 compressions, give 2 rescue breaths.

Method - Pinch the nose shut, take a normal breath, cover the person's mouth with yours, and blow until you see the chest rise. If you are not trained or uncomfortable giving breaths, continue with chest compressions only.

Continue CPR
Continue cycles of 30 compressions and 2 breaths until medical help arrives, an AED is ready to use, the person shows signs of life, or you are too exhausted to continue.

Using an AED
Turn on the AED and follow its voice prompts.
Attach the AED pads to the person's bare chest as indicated.
Ensure no one is touching the person while the AED analyses the heart rhythm. Deliver a shock if advised by the AED, then resume CPR immediately after the shock.

Potential Complications of CPR and Post-Resuscitation Issues Physical Injuries
Rib Fractures and Sternum Damage:** The force of chest compressions can break ribs or the sternum.
Internal Organ Injury - Potential for damage to internal organs such as the lungs and liver.

Neurological Damage
Brain Injury - Lack of oxygen to the brain during cardiac arrest can lead to hypoxic-ischemic brain injury, resulting in cognitive deficits, motor impairments, or coma.

Post-Resuscitation Syndrome
Reperfusion Injury - The restoration of blood flow can cause additional damage to tissues and organs due to inflammatory responses.
Systemic Inflammatory Response - Can lead to multi-organ dysfunction and failure.

Cardiac Complications
Arrhythmias - Irregular heartbeats can occur after resuscitation, requiring further medical intervention.
Myocardial Dysfunction - Temporary or permanent impairment of heart function.

Respiratory Issues
Pulmonary Oedema - Fluid accumulation in the lungs due to heart dysfunction.
Aspiration Pneumonia - Inhalation of foreign material (vomit, saliva) into the lungs during or after resuscitation.

Circulatory Problems
Hypotension - Low blood pressure due to weakened heart function.
Peripheral Circulation Issues - Poor blood flow to extremities and organs.

Post-Resuscitation Care
Advanced Cardiac Life Support (ACLS)
Ongoing monitoring and treatment by healthcare professionals in a hospital setting. Use of medications and advanced interventions to stabilise heart rhythm and blood pressure.
Neurological Care
Assessment and management of brain function.
Cooling (therapeutic hypothermia) may be used to protect the brain.
Respiratory Support
Mechanical ventilation if the person cannot breathe independently. Continuous monitoring of oxygen levels.

Cardiac Monitoring

Continuous ECG monitoring to detect and treat arrhythmias. Medications to support heart function and blood pressure.

Rehabilitation

Physical therapy, occupational therapy, and speech therapy for recovery from neurological impairments.

Psychological support for emotional and cognitive recovery.

Performing CPR can save lives, but it comes with potential complications that require comprehensive medical management after resuscitation. The timely and effective delivery of CPR, followed by advanced medical care, greatly enhances the chances of recovery and reduces the risk of long-term complications.

C. DIFF COLITIS

C. diff colitis, also known as Clostridioides difficile colitis or Clostridium difficile colitis, is an infection of the colon caused by the bacterium Clostridioides difficile (C. difficile). This condition can lead to severe diarrhoea and inflammation of the colon. Here's a detailed explanation of C. diff colitis:

Causes
C. difficile bacteria are found in the environment, especially in healthcare settings like hospitals and nursing homes. The infection usually occurs after the use of antibiotics, which can disrupt the normal gut flora and allow C. difficile to overgrow and produce toxins that cause inflammation and damage to the colon lining.

Risk Factors
Antibiotic Use - Broad-spectrum antibiotics, which kill a wide range of bacteria, are a major risk factor because they disrupt the balance of normal gut flora.
Hospitalisation or Long-term Care - Being in a healthcare setting increases exposure to C. difficile spores.
Age - Older adults are at higher risk.
Underlying Health Conditions - Having a weakened immune system or conditions such as inflammatory bowel disease (IBD).
Recent Gastrointestinal Surgery - Procedures involving the gastrointestinal tract can increase the risk.
Use of Proton Pump Inhibitors - Medications that reduce stomach acid can increase susceptibility to C. difficile.

Symptoms
Diarrhoea - Frequent, watery stools are the most common symptom.
Abdominal Pain - Cramping and tenderness in the lower abdomen.
Fever - Mild to severe fever may occur.
Nausea - Sometimes accompanied by vomiting.
Loss of Appetite - Reduced desire to eat.

Severe Cases - Can lead to dehydration, severe inflammation (pseudomembranous colitis), toxic megacolon, perforation of the colon, and sepsis.

Diagnosis
Stool Tests - Detect toxins produced by C. difficile or the presence of the bacteria itself.
Imaging - Abdominal X-rays or CT scans can identify complications like toxic megacolon.
Colonoscopy or Sigmoidoscopy - Direct visualisation of the colon to check for inflammation and pseudomembranes.

Treatment
Antibiotics
Metronidazole (Flagyl) - Often used for mild to moderate cases.
Vancomycin (Vancocin) - Commonly used for more severe cases or when metronidazole is ineffective.
Fidaxomicin (Dificid) - Another option for treating C. difficile, especially for recurrent infections.
Probiotics - May help restore normal gut flora, though their efficacy is still being studied.
Fecal Microbiota Transplant (FMT) - Transplanting stool from a healthy donor to the patient's colon to restore healthy bacteria.
Supportive Care - Includes maintaining hydration and electrolyte balance.
Surgery - In severe cases, such as toxic megacolon or perforation, surgical intervention may be required.

Prevention
Judicious Antibiotic Use - Avoid unnecessary use of antibiotics.
Infection Control in Healthcare Settings - Rigorous hand hygiene, use of personal protective equipment, and cleaning protocols to prevent the spread of C. difficile.
Probiotics - May be considered in certain cases to prevent C. difficile infection during antibiotic treatment.
Isolating Infected Patients - To prevent transmission to others.

Complications

Recurrence - Up to 20% of patients may experience recurrent infections.

Severe Colitis - Can lead to life-threatening conditions like toxic megacolon and sepsis.

Dehydration and Electrolyte Imbalance - Resulting from severe diarrhoea.

C. diff colitis is a serious condition that requires prompt diagnosis and treatment. Preventive measures, especially in healthcare settings, are crucial to control its spread. If you suspect you have symptoms of C. diff colitis, seek medical attention immediately.

CHEMOTHERAPY SIDE EFFECTS

Chemotherapy is a type of cancer treatment that uses drugs to kill cancer cells or stop them from growing and dividing. Here's a detailed overview:

How Chemotherapy Works
Targeting Rapidly Dividing Cells:
Cancer cells divide more rapidly than most normal cells. Chemotherapy drugs target these rapidly dividing cells. However, because some normal cells also divide quickly (such as those in the bone marrow, digestive tract, and hair follicles), chemotherapy can also affect these cells, leading to side effects.

Mechanism of Action:
Alkylating agents: These drugs work by directly damaging DNA to prevent the cancer cell from reproducing.

Antimetabolites: These mimic the building blocks of DNA and RNA, interfering with cell division.

Anti-tumor antibiotics: These bind with DNA and inhibit RNA synthesis, a crucial step in the cell cycle.

Topoisomerase inhibitors: These interfere with the enzymes that help separate the strands of DNA, necessary for cell division.

Mitotic inhibitors: These block the cell division process.

Administration of Chemotherapy
Routes of Administration
Intravenous (IV): Injected directly into a vein.

Oral: Taken by mouth in pill or liquid form.

Injection: Administered into a muscle (intramuscular) or under the skin (subcutaneous).

Intrathecal: Injected into the cerebrospinal fluid.

Intraperitoneal: Delivered into the abdominal cavity.

Topical: Applied to the skin.

Treatment Schedules
Chemotherapy is usually given in cycles, with periods of treatment followed by periods of rest. This allows the body time to recover from the drugs' effects.

Uses of Chemotherapy
Primary Treatment: - Used alone to cure cancer, control its growth, or alleviate symptoms.

Adjuvant Therapy:- Given after surgery or radiation to eliminate any remaining cancer cells.

Neoadjuvant Therapy:- Administered before surgery or radiation to shrink tumours.

Palliative Treatment:- Used to relieve symptoms and improve the quality of life in advanced stages of cancer.

Side Effects of Chemotherapy

Common Side Effects:
- Fatigue
- Hair loss
- Nausea and vomiting
- Diarrhea or constipation
- Mouth sores
- Increased risk of infection
- Anemia
- Bruising and bleeding easily

Long-term Side Effects:
- Damage to the heart, lungs, nerves, kidneys, or reproductive organs.
- Risk of developing a second cancer later in life.

Managing Side Effects
Medications: Anti-nausea drugs, pain relievers, and other medications can help manage side effects.

Lifestyle Adjustments: Nutrition, exercise, and rest can aid in coping with the treatment.

Support Services: Counseling, support groups, and other resources can provide emotional and practical support.

Advancements in Chemotherapy
Targeted Therapy: Drugs designed to target specific molecules involved in cancer growth.

Immunotherapy: Boosts the body's immune system to fight cancer.

Combination Therapy: Using chemotherapy in combination with other treatments such as surgery, radiation, and newer therapies to improve outcomes.

Chemotherapy has evolved significantly and continues to be a cornerstone in cancer treatment, often combined with other modalities for more effective management and potential cure of various cancers.

Chemotherapy for Breast Cancer
Chemotherapy is a common treatment for breast cancer, utilized to kill cancer cells or prevent their growth and spread. Here's a

detailed explanation of how chemotherapy is used in the context of breast cancer:

Objectives of Chemotherapy in Breast Cancer
Neoadjuvant Chemotherapy:
- Given before surgery to shrink large tumors, making them easier to remove and increasing the likelihood of breast-conserving surgery (lumpectomy) instead of mastectomy.

Adjuvant Chemotherapy:
- Administered after surgery to eliminate any remaining cancer cells, thereby reducing the risk of recurrence.

Treatment for Metastatic Breast Cancer:
- Used when cancer has spread to other parts of the body, aiming to control the disease, alleviate symptoms, and improve quality of life.

Chemotherapy Drugs Used for Breast Cancer
Anthracyclines:
- Examples: Doxorubicin (Adriamycin), Epirubicin (Ellence)
- Mechanism: Interfere with enzymes involved in DNA replication.

Taxanes:
- Examples: Paclitaxel (Taxol), Docetaxel (Taxotere)
- Mechanism: Disrupt microtubule function, hindering cell division.

Antimetabolites:
- Examples: 5-Fluorouracil (5-FU), Capecitabine (Xeloda)
- Mechanism: Mimic natural substances needed by cells, interfering with DNA and RNA synthesis.

Alkylating Agents:
- Examples: Cyclophosphamide (Cytoxan)
- Mechanism: Directly damage DNA to prevent cell division.

Platinum Agents:
- Examples: Carboplatin, Cisplatin
- Mechanism: Create cross-links in DNA, hindering replication.

Administration of Chemotherapy for Breast Cancer
Intravenous (IV): - The most common route, administered directly into the bloodstream.
Oral: - Some drugs can be taken as pills or liquids.

Treatment Schedules
- Chemotherapy is typically given in cycles, which consist of a period of treatment followed by a period of rest. This allows the body to recover from the side effects.
- The specific schedule and duration depend on the individual's treatment plan and the drugs used.

Side Effects
Short-term Side Effects:
- Fatigue
- Hair loss
- Nausea and vomiting
- Appetite changes
- Diarrhea or constipation
- Mouth sores
- Increased risk of infection
- Anemia
- Bruising and bleeding easily

Long-term Side Effects:
- Possible damage to the heart, lungs, nerves, or reproductive organs.
- Risk of secondary cancers.

Managing Side Effects
Medications: - Anti-nausea drugs, growth factors to boost blood cell counts, and other supportive medications.
Lifestyle Adjustments: - Proper nutrition, exercise, and rest.
Support Services: - Counselling, support groups, and

educational resources.

Considerations and Advancements

Molecular and Genetic Testing: - Tests such as Oncotype DX or MammaPrint can help predict the benefit of chemotherapy and guide treatment decisions.

Targeted Therapy: - Drugs such as trastuzumab (Herceptin) and pertuzumab (Perjeta) are used for HER2-positive breast cancers in combination with chemotherapy.

Hormonal Therapy: - Often combined with chemotherapy for hormone receptor-positive breast cancers to block hormones that fuel cancer growth.

Personalized Treatment - Breast cancer treatment is highly individualized. Factors such as the cancer's stage, grade, hormone receptor status, HER2 status, and the patient's overall health influence the chemotherapy regimen chosen.

Chemotherapy remains a key component in the multidisciplinary approach to treating breast cancer, often in combination with surgery, radiation therapy, hormonal therapy, and targeted therapies, aiming to optimize outcomes and improve survival rates.

Chemotherapy Side Effects
Chemotherapy for breast cancer can cause a range of side effects, which vary depending on the specific drugs used, the dosage, and individual patient factors.

Common side effects include: I developed 1 - 2 - 3 - 4 - 5 - 6 - 7 - 8 - 9 - 10 - 11 - 12 -17
    1. Fatigue: One of the most common side effects, often described as an overwhelming sense of tiredness.
    2. Nausea and Vomiting: Can be managed with anti-nausea medications.
    3. Hair Loss: Usually temporary, hair generally starts to

regrow after treatment ends.

4. Infection Risk: Due to lowered white blood cell counts (neutropenia), patients are more susceptible to infections.

5. Anaemia: Reduced red blood cell count can cause fatigue and weakness.

6. Appetite Changes: Patients may experience loss of appetite or changes in taste.

7. Mouth Sores: Sores or ulcers in the mouth or throat.

8. Diarrhoea or Constipation: Digestive issues can occur as a side effect.

9. Neuropathy: Numbness, tingling, or pain in the hands and feet caused by nerve damage.

10. Cognitive Changes: Sometimes referred to as "chemo brain," involving memory and concentration issues.

11. Skin and Nail Changes: Dry skin, changes in nail colour, or other skin reactions.

12. Weight Changes: Both weight gain and loss can occur.

13. Menstrual Changes: Chemotherapy can affect menstrual cycles and potentially lead to early menopause.

14. Fertility Issues: Can impact fertility temporarily or permanently.

15. Heart Problems: Certain chemotherapy drugs can affect heart function.

16. Bone Density Loss: Increased risk of osteoporosis.

17. Psychological Effects: Anxiety, depression, and emotional distress.

It's important for patients to discuss potential side effects with their healthcare team, as many side effects can be managed or mitigated with proper care and medication.

COLD-CAP TREATMENT

Cold cap treatment, also known as scalp cooling, is a method used to prevent or reduce hair loss (alopecia) during chemotherapy. This treatment involves wearing a specially designed cap filled with a cooling agent before, during, and after chemotherapy sessions. The cold temperature constricts the blood vessels in the scalp, reducing the amount of chemotherapy drugs that reach the hair follicles.

Here's a detailed explanation of how cold cap treatment works, the process involved, its effectiveness, and potential side effects:

How Cold Cap Treatment Works
Mechanism
Vasoconstriction - The cold temperature causes the blood vessels in the scalp to constrict (vasoconstriction), which limits the blood flow and, consequently, the amount of chemotherapy drugs reaching the hair follicles.

Reduced Metabolic Activity - The cooling also slows down the metabolic activity of the hair follicles, making them less susceptible to the damaging effects of chemotherapy.

Minimised Drug Diffusion - By reducing the temperature of the scalp, the diffusion of the chemotherapy drugs into the hair follicle cells is minimised, helping to preserve the hair.

The Process of Cold Cap Treatment
Preparation
Fitting - Before starting chemotherapy, the patient is fitted with a cold cap. The cap needs to be snug to ensure even cooling across the entire scalp.

Pre-Cooling - The cap is applied approximately 30 minutes before the chemotherapy infusion begins. This pre-cooling period helps to lower the scalp temperature adequately before the chemotherapy drugs enter the bloodstream.

During Chemotherapy

Wearing the Cap - The patient continues to wear the cold cap throughout the chemotherapy session. Depending on the type of cooling system used, the cap may need to be changed or re-cooled periodically to maintain the correct temperature.

Monitoring - The healthcare team monitors the patient for any signs of discomfort or adverse reactions.

Post-Cooling

Extended Cooling - After the chemotherapy infusion ends, the patient must continue wearing the cold cap for an additional period (usually between 1 and 2 hours) to ensure the scalp remains cool as the chemotherapy drugs are cleared from the bloodstream.

Effectiveness of Cold Cap Treatment
Success Rates

Variability - The effectiveness of cold cap treatment can vary depending on several factors, including the type of chemotherapy drugs used, the dosage, and individual patient differences.

Success Rates - Studies have shown that scalp cooling can significantly reduce hair loss in many patients. Success rates range from 50% to over 70%, with some patients experiencing only partial hair loss and others maintaining most of their hair.

Factors Influencing Effectiveness

Chemotherapy Regimen - Certain chemotherapy drugs are more likely to cause hair loss, and the effectiveness of scalp cooling may be reduced with these agents.

Individual Differences - Factors such as hair thickness, hair type, and scalp conditions can also influence the outcome.

Potential Side Effects and Considerations
Side Effects

Discomfort - Some patients may experience discomfort or headaches due to the cold temperature of the cap. This discomfort often diminishes after the first few sessions as patients become accustomed to the treatment.

Cold Sensation - A strong cold sensation on the scalp is common, and some patients may find this sensation difficult to tolerate.

Considerations

Time Commitment - Cold cap treatment requires additional time before, during, and after chemotherapy sessions, which can extend the overall duration of each treatment visit.

Not Universally Effective - While many patients benefit from cold cap treatment, it is not universally effective, and some patients may still experience significant hair loss.

Post-Treatment Hair Care

Gentle Handling - Patients are often advised to handle their hair gently, avoiding excessive brushing, heat styling, or harsh chemical treatments to minimise additional hair loss.

Mild Products - Using mild shampoos and conditioners can help protect the hair and scalp.

Cold cap treatment is a valuable option for patients undergoing chemotherapy who wish to reduce the risk of hair loss. By understanding the process, effectiveness, and potential side effects, patients can make informed decisions in consultation with their healthcare providers about whether this treatment is suitable for them.

DEXA

A DEXA scan, also known as dual-energy X-ray absorptiometry scan, is a medical imaging test used to measure bone mineral density (BMD). It's primarily used to diagnose and monitor conditions like osteoporosis and assess the risk of fractures.

Here's a detailed explanation of what a DEXA scan involves, its purpose, and the procedure:

Purpose of a DEXA Scan
Diagnose Osteoporosis - To detect osteoporosis, a condition where bones become weak and brittle.
Fracture Risk Assessment - To estimate the risk of fractures, especially in postmenopausal women and older adults.
Monitor Bone Density - To monitor changes in bone density over time, especially in patients undergoing treatment for osteoporosis or other conditions affecting bone health.
Evaluate Bone Health - To assess bone health in patients with certain conditions such as chronic kidney disease, endocrine disorders, or those taking medications that affect bone density.

How a DEXA Scan Works
A DEXA scan uses two X-ray beams at different energy levels. When the beams pass through the body, the machine measures the amount of X-rays that are absorbed by the bones. This information is used to calculate bone density. The two energy levels help differentiate between bone and soft tissue, providing a precise measurement of bone density.

Procedure for a DEXA Scan
Preparation
Clothing - Wear loose, comfortable clothing without metal zippers, belts, or buttons. You may be asked to change into a hospital gown.
Avoid Calcium Supplements - Do not take calcium supplements for at least 24 hours before the scan.
Medical History - Inform the technologist if you recently had

any barium exams or contrast material used in CT scans or nuclear medicine tests, as these might interfere with the DEXA scan.

During the Scan
Positioning - You will lie on your back on a padded table. The technician may position your legs using a padded block to flatten the lower spine or place your arms at your sides to ensure proper alignment.

Scanning - The DEXA machine passes over your body, usually focusing on the hip and spine, the most common sites for measuring bone density. You must lie still during the scan to ensure accurate results.

Duration - The scan typically takes about 10-20 minutes and is painless.

After the Scan
No Recovery Time - You can resume normal activities immediately after the scan.

Results - A radiologist or a specialist will analyse the results and send a report to your doctor. The results will include T-scores and Z-scores.

Understanding the Results
- Score - Compares your bone density to the average peak bone density of a healthy young adult of the same sex.

+1 to -1 - Normal bone density

-1 to -2.5 - Low bone density (osteopenia)

-2.5 and below - Osteoporosis

Z-score - Compares your bone density to the average bone density of people your age, sex, and size.

A Z-score below 2.0 might indicate that something other than aging is causing abnormal bone loss.

Benefits and Risks
Benefits
Non-invasive and painless.

Quick and accurate assessment of bone density.

Low radiation exposure.

Risks

Minimal radiation exposure, which is generally considered safe. However, it may not be recommended for pregnant women due to potential risks to the foetus.

A DEXA scan is a valuable tool for assessing bone health, diagnosing osteoporosis, and helping guide treatment decisions. Always consult with your healthcare provider to understand your specific needs and the implications of the test results.

DNR - DO NOT RESUSCITATE ORDER

A Do Not Resuscitate (DNR) order is a legal document that communicates a patient's wish to forgo cardiopulmonary resuscitation (CPR) and advanced cardiac life support (ACLS) in the event of cardiac or respiratory arrest. The purpose of a DNR is to respect the patient's autonomy and ensure that their end-of-life preferences are honoured. Here's a detailed explanation of the purpose and implications of a DNR:

Purpose of a DNR
Respecting Patient Autonomy
Allows individuals to make informed decisions about their own healthcare. Ensures that patients can choose not to undergo potentially invasive and traumatic procedures.
Preventing Unwanted Interventions
Avoids aggressive medical treatments that the patient may find unacceptable or that may not align with their values and quality of life considerations.
Helps prevent unnecessary suffering for patients with terminal illnesses or severe, irreversible medical conditions.
Quality of Life Considerations
Prioritises the patient's comfort and dignity at the end of life.
Focuses on palliative care and symptom management rather than life-prolonging measures that may not improve the patient's overall well-being.
Clarity for Healthcare Providers
Provides clear instructions to medical personnel, ensuring that the patient's wishes are followed.
Reduces ambiguity and potential conflicts among family members and healthcare teams during critical moments.
Facilitating End-of-Life Planning
Encourages discussions about end-of-life care preferences between patients, families, and healthcare providers.
Integrates into broader advance care planning, including living wills and healthcare power of attorney documents.

How a DNR is Implemented

Creating a DNR Order

Initiated by the patient or their legal representative in consultation with a physician. A physician must sign the DNR order to make it valid.

Can be part of a broader advance directive or a standalone document.

Documentation

DNR orders should be clearly documented in the patient's medical record. Copies of the DNR should be readily accessible at home, especially for patients receiving home care or residing in assisted living facilities.

Communication

The patient's healthcare providers, including emergency medical personnel, should be informed of the DNR order.

Family members and caregivers should also be aware of the patient's wishes.

Implications of a DNR

During Medical Emergencies

If the patient experiences cardiac or respiratory arrest, no attempts are made to restart the heart or breathing.

Other medical treatments and interventions unrelated to resuscitation may still be provided unless otherwise specified in the patient's advance directives.

Scope of DNR Orders

A DNR specifically addresses CPR and ACLS. It does not mean the patient will not receive other forms of medical care, such as pain management, antibiotics, or other treatments to improve quality of life.

Revoking a DNR

Patients have the right to change their minds and revoke a DNR order at any time. The revocation should be communicated to the healthcare team and documented in the medical record.

Ethical and Legal Considerations

Ensures that the healthcare team respects the patient's right to refuse life-sustaining treatment.

Protects healthcare providers from legal liability when they honour the DNR order, as long as it is properly documented and communicated.

Challenges and Considerations
Emotional and Ethical Challenges
Discussions about DNR orders can be emotionally difficult for patients and families. Ethical dilemmas may arise if family members disagree with the patient's wishes.

Misunderstandings and Miscommunication
There may be misunderstandings about the scope and implications of a DNR order. Clear and compassionate communication is essential to ensure everyone understands the patient's preferences.

Variability in Regulations
Regulations and policies regarding DNR orders can vary by region and healthcare institution.
It is important to ensure that the DNR order complies with local laws and hospital policies.

A DNR order is a critical component of advance care planning that ensures a patient's end-of-life preferences are respected. It aims to provide clarity, prevent unnecessary interventions, and prioritise the patient's comfort and dignity during their final moments.

ECG

An electrocardiogram (ECG or EKG) is a non-invasive medical test that records the electrical activity of the heart over a period of time. It is a crucial tool in diagnosing and monitoring various heart conditions.

Here's an in-depth explanation of what an ECG is and the purpose of having one:

What is an ECG?
Definition
An ECG is a test that measures the electrical signals produced by the heart as it beats. These signals are displayed as a series of waves on a monitor or printed on paper.

Components of an ECG
Electrodes - Small, sticky patches placed on the skin at specific locations (chest, arms, and legs) to detect the heart's electrical activity.
Leads - Wires connecting the electrodes to the ECG machine, which amplifies and records the electrical signals.
ECG Machine - A device that records the electrical activity and displays it as waveforms.

How an ECG is Performed
Preparation
The patient is asked to lie down.
The skin where the electrodes will be placed is cleaned to ensure good contact. Electrodes are attached to the chest, arms, and legs.
Recording
The patient must remain still and breathe normally.
The ECG machine records the heart's electrical activity for a short period (usually 10 seconds).
The recorded data is displayed on a screen or printed out for analysis.
Completion

The electrodes are removed.
The entire procedure usually takes about 5 to 10 minutes

Purpose of Having an ECG
An ECG is used for various diagnostic and monitoring purposes:

Diagnosing Heart Conditions
Arrhythmias - Identifies irregular heartbeats, such as atrial fibrillation or ventricular tachycardia.
Heart Attack - Detects signs of a previous or ongoing heart attack (myocardial infarction) by identifying abnormal patterns in the ECG waves.
Coronary Artery Disease - Indicates poor blood flow to the heart muscle due to blocked or narrowed arteries.
Heart Enlargement - Shows evidence of an enlarged heart (hypertrophy), which can occur due to high blood pressure or other conditions.

Monitoring Heart Health
Post-Heart Attack - Tracks the heart's recovery and helps plan further treatment.
Medication Effects - Monitors how medications affect the heart's rhythm and function.
Chronic Conditions - Evaluates the heart's condition in patients with chronic diseases like diabetes, hypertension, or heart failure.

Pre-Surgical Assessment
Surgical Risk - Assesses heart health before major surgeries to evaluate the risk of complications.

Symptom Evaluation
Chest Pain - Investigates the cause of chest pain, which may be related to heart problems.
Shortness of Breath - Assesses whether breathing difficulties are related to heart issues.
Palpitations - Evaluates the cause of sensations of rapid or irregular heartbeats.

Understanding ECG Results
Normal ECG
Shows a regular pattern of P waves, QRS complexes, and T waves. Indicates normal heart rhythm and function.
Abnormal ECG
Deviations from the normal pattern may suggest various heart conditions.

ST-Segment Changes - Elevation or depression can indicate a heart attack or ischemia.

T-Wave Abnormalities - May suggest electrolyte imbalances, ischemia, or other issues.

Prolonged Intervals - Abnormalities in the PR, QRS, or QT intervals can indicate conduction problems.

Conclusion
An ECG is a vital diagnostic tool that provides crucial information about the heart's electrical activity. It helps diagnose and monitor a wide range of heart conditions, guide treatment decisions, and assess the overall health of the heart. The procedure is quick, non-invasive, and highly informative, making it an essential part of cardiovascular care.

ENDOCRINE

Endocrine treatment, also known as hormone therapy, involves manipulating the body's hormone levels to treat various medical conditions. This type of treatment is commonly used in the management of hormone-sensitive cancers, such as breast and prostate cancer, as well as in treating endocrine disorders like hypothyroidism, hyperthyroidism, and diabetes. Here's a detailed explanation of how endocrine treatment works:

Breast Cancer
Mechanism - Some breast cancers are hormone receptor-positive, meaning they grow in response to hormones like oestrogen and progesterone. Endocrine treatment works by lowering hormone levels or blocking their effects on cancer cells.

Medications
Selective Oestrogen Receptor Modulators (SERMs) - Drugs like tamoxifen block oestrogen receptors on breast cancer cells, preventing oestrogen from stimulating cancer growth.
Aromatase Inhibitors - Drugs like anastrozole, letrozole, and exemestane inhibit the enzyme aromatase, which converts androgens into oestrogen in postmenopausal women, thereby reducing oestrogen levels.
Oestrogen Receptor Down-regulators (ERDs) - Drugs like fulvestrant degrade oestrogen receptors, blocking oestrogen signalling in breast cancer cells. **Indications** - Used in premenopausal and postmenopausal women, often as adjuvant therapy following surgery, radiation, or chemotherapy.

Prostate Cancer
Mechanism - Prostate cancer often depends on androgens (male hormones) like testosterone for growth. Endocrine treatment reduces androgen levels or blocks their action on cancer cells.
Medications
Luteinising Hormone-Releasing Hormone (LHRH) Agonists and Antagonists - Drugs like leuprolide and degarelix lower

testosterone levels by affecting hormone signalling from the brain to the testes.

Anti-Androgens - Drugs like bicalutamide and enzalutamide block androgen receptors, preventing testosterone from stimulating prostate cancer growth. **Indications** - Used in advanced or metastatic prostate cancer, often in combination with other treatments like surgery or radiation.

Endocrine Treatment for Endocrine Disorders
Hypothyroidism

Mechanism - Hypothyroidism is a condition where the thyroid gland does not produce enough thyroid hormone. Endocrine treatment involves hormone replacement to restore normal thyroid function.

Medications

Levothyroxine - A synthetic form of the thyroid hormone thyroxine (T4), which is converted to the active form triiodothyronine (T3) in the body.

Indications - Used to normalise thyroid hormone levels, alleviate symptoms like fatigue and weight gain, and maintain metabolic balance.

Hyperthyroidism

Mechanism - Hyperthyroidism is a condition where the thyroid gland produces excessive thyroid hormone. Treatment aims to reduce hormone production or block its effects.

Medications

Antithyroid Drugs - Medications like methimazole and propylthiouracil inhibit thyroid hormone synthesis.

Beta-Blockers - Drugs like propranolol manage symptoms like rapid heart rate and tremors by blocking the effects of excess thyroid hormone.

Radioactive Iodine - Destroys overactive thyroid cells, reducing hormone production.

Indications - Used to control symptoms and normalise thyroid function, sometimes followed by thyroid hormone replacement if hypothyroidism develops.

Diabetes
Mechanism - Diabetes involves improper regulation of blood glucose levels. Endocrine treatment aims to control glucose levels and prevent complications. Medications

Insulin Therapy - Used in Type 1 diabetes and advanced Type 2 diabetes, where insulin production is inadequate. Various forms of insulin, including rapid-acting, long-acting, and intermediate-acting, are used to mimic natural insulin release.

Oral Hypoglycemics - Medications like metformin and sulfonylureas enhance insulin action or stimulate insulin secretion in Type 2 diabetes.

Indications - Aimed at achieving glycemic control, preventing complications like neuropathy, nephropathy, and retinopathy, and improving overall quality of life.

Hormone Replacement Therapy (HRT)
Menopause
Mechanism - Menopause causes a decline in oestrogen and progesterone levels, leading to symptoms like hot flashes, night sweats, and osteoporosis. HRT involves supplementing these hormones.

Medications

Oestrogen Therapy - Can be administered orally, transdermally (patches), or topically (gels, creams).

Combined Oestrogen-Progesterone Therapy - Used in women with an intact uterus to prevent endometrial hyperplasia.

Indications - Relief of menopausal symptoms, prevention of bone loss, and improvement of quality of life.

Monitoring and Side Effects
Endocrine treatments require careful monitoring to manage potential side effects and ensure effectiveness. Regular follow-ups, blood tests, and imaging studies are often necessary.

Side effects can vary depending on the treatment and may include weight gain, hot flashes, increased risk of blood clots, cardiovascular issues, and osteoporosis. Long- term hormone therapy, particularly in cancer treatment, can have significant side effects requiring management.

Endocrine treatment is a critical component in managing a variety of medical conditions, providing relief, improving quality of life, and in some cases, extending survival.

LETROZOLE

Letrozole is a medication primarily used in the treatment of hormone receptor-positive breast cancer in postmenopausal women. It belongs to a class of drugs known as aromatase inhibitors.

Reasons for Taking Letrozole:
   Breast Cancer Treatment - Letrozole is used to treat hormone receptor-positive breast cancer, which relies on estrogen to grow. By lowering estrogen levels in the body, letrozole helps to slow or stop the growth of these cancer cells.
   Prevention of Recurrence - After initial treatment for breast cancer (such as surgery or radiation), letrozole can be prescribed to prevent the cancer from returning.
   Fertility Treatment - In some cases, letrozole is used off-label to induce ovulation in women with polycystic ovary syndrome (PCOS) or other ovulatory disorders.

Side Effects of Letrozole:
   Common Side Effects: I developed 1 - 2 - 3 - 5 - 6 - 7
1. **Hot Flashes** - A common side effect due to the reduction of estrogen.
2. **Joint Pain and Muscle Pain** - Often reported by patients.
3. **Fatigue** - Many users experience increased tiredness.
4. **Nausea** - Some patients may feel nauseous.
5. **Headache** - A relatively common complaint.
6. **Increased Sweating** - Night sweats and increased perspiration can occur.
7. **Weight Gain** - Some users report gaining weight while on the medication.

Less Common Side Effects: I developed 1 - 3 - 4 - 5
1. **Bone Pain** - Letrozole can cause bone pain or exacerbate osteoporosis.
2. **High Cholesterol** - Changes in cholesterol levels can occur.
3. **Hair Thinning** - Some patients may notice hair loss or thinning.
4. **Depression and Mood Changes** - Emotional and psychological side effects are possible.
5. **Dizziness** - A feeling of lightheadedness or dizziness can be experienced.
6. **Swelling of Legs or Arms (Edema)** - Fluid retention leading to swelling is possible.

Serious Side Effects (Require medical attention):

1. **Severe Bone, Joint, or Muscle Pain** - Intense pain can be debilitating.
2. **Signs of Liver Problems** - Yellowing of the skin or eyes, dark urine, severe nausea or vomiting.
3. **Severe Allergic Reactions** - Rash, itching, swelling, severe dizziness, trouble breathing.
4. **Heart Issues** - Increased risk of heart problems, particularly in those with pre-existing conditions.

Mechanism of Action:
Letrozole inhibits the enzyme aromatase, which converts androgens into estrogen in postmenopausal women. By blocking this conversion, letrozole significantly reduces estrogen levels, thereby slowing the growth of estrogen receptor-positive breast cancer cells.

Conclusion:
While letrozole is an effective treatment for hormone receptor-positive breast cancer and has potential uses in fertility treatments, it does come with a range of potential side effects. Patients should discuss the benefits and risks with their healthcare provider to ensure it is the right treatment for their condition. Regular monitoring and communication with a healthcare provider can help manage and mitigate these side effects.

LUMPECTOMY

A lumpectomy, also known as breast-conserving surgery or partial mastectomy, is a surgical procedure performed to remove a cancerous tumour from the breast along with a small margin of surrounding healthy tissue. This approach aims to eliminate the cancer while preserving as much of the breast as possible. Here's an overview of the procedure, its purpose, and what patients can expect:

Purpose
Cancer Removal - The primary goal of a lumpectomy is to excise the breast cancer tumour while maintaining the appearance and functionality of the breast.

Diagnosis Confirmation - The removed tissue is analysed to confirm the type, grade, and extent of cancer.

Procedure
Preoperative Preparation
Consultation - The patient meets with the surgical team to discuss the procedure, risks, and benefits. Imaging tests like mammograms or ultrasounds may be used to locate the tumour precisely.

Marking the Tumour - Sometimes, a radiologist may place a small marker or wire in the tumour to guide the surgeon.

Anaesthesia
General Anaesthesia - The patient is typically under general anaesthesia, meaning they are asleep during the surgery.

Local Anaesthesia - In some cases, local anaesthesia with sedation may be used.

Surgical Process
Incision - The surgeon makes an incision in the breast over or near the tumour.

Tumour Removal - The tumour, along with a margin of surrounding healthy tissue, is carefully removed. The margin ensures that no cancer cells are left behind.

Sentinel Lymph Node Biopsy - Often performed alongside a lumpectomy, this involves removing one or a few sentinel lymph nodes (the first nodes to which cancer cells are likely to spread) to check for metastasis.

Postoperative Steps
Closure - The incision is closed with sutures or surgical glue.
Pathology - The excised tissue is sent to a pathology lab to analyse the margins and determine if any cancer cells are present at the edges.

Postoperative Care
Recovery - Most patients can go home the same day or after an overnight stay. Recovery involves managing pain, caring for the incision site, and gradually resuming normal activities.
Follow-Up - Follow-up appointments are essential to monitor healing and discuss the pathology results.

Radiation Therapy
Adjuvant Therapy - After a lumpectomy, most patients undergo radiation therapy to eliminate any remaining cancer cells and reduce the risk of recurrence.
Advantages and Considerations
Advantages
Preserves most of the breast tissue.
Offers a good cosmetic outcome.
Shorter recovery time compared to a mastectomy.
Considerations
Not suitable for all types of breast cancer. Factors like tumour size, location, and patient preference play a role.
May need additional treatments like chemotherapy, hormone therapy, or radiation.

Risks and Complications
Common Risks
Infection, bleeding, pain, swelling, and changes in breast shape or appearance.

Rare Complications
Anaesthesia reactions, delayed wound healing, or the need for additional surgery if cancer margins are not clear.

In summary, a lumpectomy is a breast-conserving surgery that removes a cancerous tumour while aiming to retain the appearance of the breast. It involves precise surgical techniques, careful postoperative care, and often follow-up treatments like radiation therapy to ensure the best possible outcome for the patient.

MAMMOGRAM

A mammogram is a specialised X-ray imaging technique used to examine the breast for any signs of abnormalities, including breast cancer. It is a key tool in breast cancer screening and diagnosis.

Purpose
Screening - Mammograms are routinely used to screen for breast cancer in women who have no symptoms. The goal is to detect cancer early when it is most treatable.

Diagnostic - When a lump or other symptom of breast cancer is detected, a diagnostic mammogram helps to further investigate these abnormalities.

Types of Mammograms
Screening Mammogram - Typically performed on women who have no symptoms of breast cancer. It involves taking two X-ray images of each breast to detect tumours that cannot be felt.

Diagnostic Mammogram - Used when there are symptoms such as a lump, pain, nipple discharge, or after an abnormal screening mammogram. This type of mammogram takes more detailed images from multiple angles.

Procedure
Preparation
Appointment Scheduling - Often scheduled for one week after the menstrual period to reduce discomfort.

Avoid Certain Products - On the day of the exam, patients should avoid using deodorants, powders, or lotions under their arms or on their breasts as these can appear on the mammogram and interfere with the results.

During the Mammogram
Positioning - The patient stands in front of the mammography machine. A technologist helps position the breast on the machine's plate.

Compression - Another plate compresses the breast to flatten the tissue. This compression is essential for obtaining clear images and minimising radiation exposure. It can be uncomfortable but lasts only a few seconds.

Imaging - X-ray images are taken, usually two per breast from different angles. The technologist checks the images for clarity before the patient leaves.

Interpretation

Radiologist Review - A radiologist examines the images for any signs of abnormalities such as masses, calcifications, or asymmetries.

Results - The results are typically sent to the patient and their healthcare provider. If anything suspicious is found, additional imaging tests or a biopsy may be recommended.

Benefits

Early Detection - Mammograms can detect breast cancer early, even before it can be felt, significantly increasing the chances of successful treatment.

Reduced Mortality - Regular mammograms have been shown to reduce the risk of dying from breast cancer among women aged 40 to 74, especially those over 50.

Risks and Limitations

Radiation Exposure - Mammograms involve a small amount of radiation exposure, but the benefits of early cancer detection outweigh the risks for most women.

False Positives/Negatives - Sometimes, mammograms can suggest cancer when there is none (false positive) or miss cancer that is present (false negative). This can lead to unnecessary anxiety or a delay in diagnosis.

Discomfort - Some women experience discomfort or pain during the compression phase of the procedure.

Recommendations

Screening Guidelines - Different organisations have varying guidelines, but many recommend regular screening mammograms starting at age 40 to 50, continuing annually or biennially. Women with higher risk factors, such as a family history of breast cancer, may need to start earlier.

In summary, a mammogram is a crucial imaging tool for the early detection and diagnosis of breast cancer, involving a low-dose X-ray of the breast. While it can cause some discomfort and involves minor radiation exposure, its benefits in identifying breast cancer early and reducing mortality are significant. Regular screenings are recommended based on age and risk factors.

MAMMOPLASTY

Mammoplasty, or breast surgery, is commonly performed for both therapeutic and reconstructive purposes in the context of breast cancer. There are several types of mammoplasty procedures that may be utilised depending on the individual's diagnosis, the extent of cancer, and personal preferences. Here's an overview of the main types of mammoplasty related to breast cancer:

Types of Mammoplasty for Cancer
Lumpectomy (Breast-Conserving Surgery)**:
Purpose - Removes the cancerous tumour and a small margin of surrounding healthy tissue while preserving most of the breast.
Procedure - Typically involves making an incision over the tumour site, excising the tumour, and then closing the incision.
Follow-Up - Often followed by radiation therapy to eliminate any remaining cancer cells and reduce the risk of recurrence.

Mastectomy
Purpose - Removes the entire breast to eliminate or reduce the risk of breast cancer.

Types
Total (Simple) Mastectomy - Removal of the entire breast, including the nipple, areola, and most of the overlying skin.
Modified Radical Mastectomy - Includes removal of the entire breast and most of the lymph nodes under the arm (axillary lymph nodes).
Radical Mastectomy - Rarely performed, this procedure involves removing the entire breast, axillary lymph nodes, and chest wall muscles under the breast.
Skin-Sparing Mastectomy - Removes breast tissue, nipple, and areola but preserves most of the skin over the breast. Often used when immediate reconstruction is planned.
Nipple-Sparing Mastectomy - Removes breast tissue but preserves the nipple and areola. Suitable for selected patients,

typically followed by reconstruction.

Reconstructive Mammoplasty
Purpose - Restores the shape and appearance of the breast following mastectomy or lumpectomy.

Types
Implant-Based Reconstruction - Involves the insertion of a saline or silicone implant to recreate the breast mound.
Autologous Tissue Reconstruction (Flap Surgery) - Uses the patient's own tissue from another part of the body (such as the abdomen, back, or thighs) to form a new breast.
Combination Reconstruction - Combines implants and autologous tissue to achieve the desired breast shape and size.

Timing
Immediate Reconstruction - Performed at the same time as the mastectomy.
Delayed Reconstruction - Performed after recovery from mastectomy and any additional treatments such as radiation or chemotherapy.

Considerations for Mammoplasty in Cancer Treatment
Cancer Stage and Type - The extent and type of cancer will influence the choice of surgery. Early-stage cancers might be treated with lumpectomy, while more extensive disease may require mastectomy.
Patient's Health and Preferences - The patient's overall health, personal preferences, and lifestyle considerations play a significant role in choosing the type of surgery and reconstruction.
Breast Size and Shape - The size and shape of the breast can affect the type of reconstructive surgery that is most appropriate.
Radiation Therapy - Patients who will undergo radiation therapy may have specific considerations, as radiation can affect the timing and type of reconstructive surgery.
Genetic Factors - Patients with genetic predispositions (e.g., BRCA1 or BRCA2 mutations) might opt for prophylactic mastectomy to reduce the risk of developing breast cancer.

Potential Complications and Side Effects

Infection - As with any surgery, there is a risk of infection at the surgical site.

Bleeding and Hematoma - Accumulation of blood at the surgical site may require intervention.

Scarring - Surgical scars are inevitable, and their extent can vary.

Pain and Discomfort - Post-operative pain and discomfort are common but usually manageable with medication.

Changes in Sensation - There may be changes in sensation in the breast or donor site (for flap procedures).

Reconstruction Complications - Potential issues include implant rupture, flap failure, or asymmetry.

Recovery and Follow-Up

Post-Operative Care - Includes wound care, managing pain, and monitoring for any signs of complications.

Physical Therapy - May be recommended to restore range of motion and strength, especially after mastectomy with lymph node removal.

Regular Follow-Up - Essential for monitoring healing, assessing for any recurrence of cancer, and managing long-term effects of surgery and reconstruction.

Emotional and Psychological Support

Breast cancer surgery can have a significant emotional and psychological impact. Counselling, support groups, and resources for coping with body image changes are important aspects of comprehensive cancer care.

In conclusion, mammoplasty for breast cancer involves various surgical options tailored to treat the cancer effectively while considering the patient's preferences and overall health. Collaboration between oncologists, surgeons, and plastic surgeons is crucial to achieve the best outcomes for the patient.

NEGATIVE PRESSURE DRESSING

A portable negative pressure dressing, also known as a portable negative pressure wound therapy (NPWT) device, is used to promote wound healing by creating a controlled negative pressure environment at the wound site. Here's a detailed description of how it works and why it's used:

How It Works
Application
Wound Dressing - A special foam or gauze dressing is placed directly onto the wound. This dressing conforms to the wound bed, ensuring even distribution of pressure.
Sealing - The wound dressing is then covered with an airtight, adhesive film that seals the wound area, creating a controlled environment.
Connection to the Device
A tube connects the dressing to a portable pump device. The tube allows for the transfer of fluids from the wound to a canister or reservoir within the device.
Negative Pressure Application
The portable device generates negative pressure (a vacuum) which is transmitted through the tube to the wound dressing.
The level of negative pressure is usually adjustable, allowing for customisation based on the wound type and patient's needs.
Fluid Removal
The negative pressure pulls exudate (fluid) and debris from the wound into the dressing and then through the tube into the canister.
This helps keep the wound clean and prevents the accumulation of fluids that could lead to infection.
Wound Contraction
The negative pressure draws the edges of the wound together, promoting faster and more effective closure of the wound.
Stimulation of Healing
The vacuum environment promotes increased blood flow to the wound area, providing essential nutrients and oxygen.

It also stimulates the formation of granulation tissue, a key component in the wound healing process.

Reasons for Its Use
Enhanced Healing
By maintaining a moist wound environment and continuously removing exudate, NPWT promotes a faster and more efficient healing process.

Infection Prevention
Continuous removal of wound exudate reduces the risk of infection by preventing bacterial colonisation and growth in the wound area.

Reduced Swelling and Oedema
The negative pressure helps to reduce local swelling and oedema, which can impede healing if left unchecked.

Improved Blood Flow
The vacuum effect increases local blood circulation, ensuring that the wound site receives ample oxygen and nutrients necessary for tissue repair.

Convenience and Mobility
Being portable, these devices allow patients to continue their daily activities while receiving continuous wound therapy. This is particularly beneficial for patients with chronic wounds or those requiring long-term wound care.

Versatility
Portable NPWT devices can be used for a variety of wounds including acute, chronic, traumatic, and surgical wounds. They are also effective in treating wounds with significant tissue loss or those with a high risk of complications.

By providing a controlled, sterile environment that supports and accelerates the natural wound healing processes, portable negative pressure dressings represent a significant advancement in wound care management.

PERIPHERALLY INSERTED CENTRAL CATHETER (PICC) LINE

A Peripherally Inserted Central Catheter (PICC) line is a long, flexible tube that is inserted into a peripheral vein, typically in the arm, and advanced through larger veins until the tip rests in a large vein near the heart. Here's a detailed explanation of how a PICC line is fitted:

Preparation
Before the procedure, the healthcare provider will explain the process to the patient and address any concerns. The patient might be asked to lie down with their arm extended. The insertion site, usually in the upper arm, is selected based on the patient's anatomy and vein accessibility. The area is then cleaned thoroughly with an antiseptic solution to minimise the risk of infection.

Insertion
The healthcare provider will use an ultrasound device to locate a suitable vein for insertion. Once the vein is identified, a local anaesthetic is administered to numb the area. This helps to minimise discomfort during the procedure. A small needle is then inserted into the vein, and a guide wire is threaded through the needle into the vein. The needle is removed, leaving the guide wire in place.

Advancing the Catheter
A dilator and sheath are placed over the guide wire to help widen the vein. The PICC line catheter is then threaded over the guide wire and advanced through the sheath into the vein. The catheter is carefully pushed along the vein until the tip reaches the large vein near the heart (the superior vena cava or the right atrium). The guide wire and sheath are then removed, leaving the catheter in place.

Securing and Dressing
Once the catheter is correctly positioned, its placement is

usually confirmed with a chest X-ray or fluoroscopy to ensure that the tip is in the proper location. The catheter is then secured to the skin with a securement device or sutures to prevent it from moving. A sterile dressing is applied over the insertion site to keep it clean and protect it from infection. The external part of the catheter has a clamp to close off the line when not in use and a cap for attaching IV medications or fluids.

Post-Procedure Care

After the PICC line is fitted, the patient and their caregivers are given instructions on how to care for the line. This includes keeping the dressing clean and dry, flushing the catheter to maintain patency, and monitoring for signs of infection or complications. Regular follow-up appointments are typically scheduled to check the condition of the PICC line and address any issues that may arise.

Fitting a PICC line is a minimally invasive procedure that provides a reliable way to administer medications, nutrients, or draw blood over an extended period, making it particularly useful for patients requiring long-term intravenous therapy.

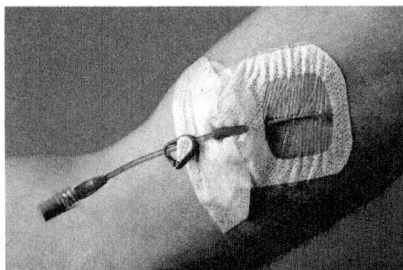

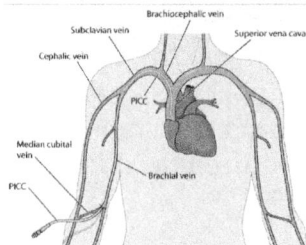

Picture of PICC line in-situ.   *Diagram showing*

placement of PICC line.

Procedure for cleaning and flushing of the PICC line
Cleaning and flushing a peripherally inserted central catheter (PICC) line is a crucial procedure to maintain its patency and prevent infection. Here's a step-by-step guide to perform these tasks:

Equipment Needed
- Alcohol or chlorhexidine wipes
- 10 ml syringes filled with sterile saline (0.9% sodium chloride)
- 10 ml syringes filled with heparin (if prescribed, usually 100 units/ml) - Sterile gloves
- Clean paper towel or drape

Preparation
Wash Hands - Thoroughly wash your hands with soap and water, or use an alcohol- based hand sanitiser.
Prepare Equipment - Gather all the necessary supplies. Place them on a clean, dry surface.
Wear Gloves - Put on sterile gloves to minimise the risk of infection.

Cleaning the PICC Line
Inspect the Site - Check the PICC insertion site for signs of infection, such as redness, swelling, or discharge. Notify a healthcare provider if any abnormalities are observed.
Clean the Cap - Use an alcohol or chlorhexidine wipe to clean the catheter cap for at least 15-30 seconds. Allow it to air dry completely before proceeding.

Flushing the PICC Line
Attach Saline Syringe - Remove the cap from the saline syringe, ensuring not to touch the tip. Attach the syringe to the PICC line by twisting it onto the access port.
Aspirate - Gently pull back on the plunger to check for blood return. This confirms the line is functioning properly. If you do not see blood return, do not proceed with the flush and contact a

healthcare provider.

Flush with Saline - Push the saline into the catheter using a pulsatile (start-stop) motion. This technique helps clear any buildup inside the line. Flush with the entire 10 ml of saline.

Detach Syringe - Once the saline has been administered, remove the syringe from the access port.

Flushing with Heparin (if prescribed)

Attach Heparin Syringe - Remove the cap from the heparin syringe and attach it to the PICC line.

Administer Heparin - Slowly inject the heparin into the catheter. The usual volume is 3-5 ml, but follow the specific instructions provided by the healthcare provider.

Detach Syringe - Remove the heparin syringe from the access port once the heparin has been administered.

Final Steps

Secure the Line - Ensure the catheter is securely clamped if it has a clamp.

Dispose of Supplies - Dispose of the used syringes and gloves in a sharps container and any other waste according to local regulations.

Wash Hands Again - Wash your hands thoroughly after completing the procedure.

Tips and Precautions

Frequency - Flushing frequency varies based on the type of PICC line and the healthcare provider's instructions, typically every 12 hours or after each use.

Volume - Always use a 10 ml syringe for flushing, as smaller syringes can create too much pressure and damage the catheter.

Sterility - Maintain a sterile technique throughout the procedure to prevent infection.

Monitor for Issues - Regularly check the PICC line and insertion site for any signs of complications and report them immediately to a healthcare provider.

Following these steps carefully helps ensure the PICC line remains functional and reduces the risk of complications. Always adhere to the specific protocols provided by your healthcare provider.

PROSTAP (LEUPRORELIN ACETATE) INJECTION

Prostap (leuprorelin acetate) is a type of medication known as a gonadotropin-releasing hormone (GnRH) agonist. It is used in various medical conditions to regulate hormone levels.

Reasons for Having a Prostap Injection:
Prostate Cancer - Prostap is used in the treatment of advanced prostate cancer. It works by reducing the levels of testosterone, which can help slow the growth of prostate cancer cells.
Endometriosis - For women, Prostap is used to manage endometriosis, a condition where tissue similar to the lining inside the uterus grows outside the uterus, causing pain and potentially infertility.
Uterine Fibroids - Prostap can be used to shrink uterine fibroids, which are non-cancerous growths in the uterus that can cause heavy menstrual bleeding, pain, and other symptoms.
Central Precocious Puberty - Prostap is used to treat children who have central precocious puberty, a condition where puberty begins too early.
Assisted Reproduction - It can be used as part of controlled ovarian stimulation protocols in assisted reproductive technology (ART) to prevent premature ovulation.

Side Effects of Prostap:
Common Side Effects: I have 1 - 2 - 3- 4 - 5 - 6 - 7
1. Hot Flashes - Similar to menopausal symptoms, due to decreased hormone levels.
2. Sweating - Increased sweating or night sweats can occur.
3. Headaches - Many patients report headaches.
4. Mood Changes - Including depression, anxiety, or irritability.
5. Decreased Libido - Reduced sexual desire is common.
6. Injection Site Reactions - Pain, redness, or swelling at the injection site.
7. Musculoskeletal Pain - Joint and muscle pain may occur.

Less Common Side Effects: I have 1 - 2 - 3 - 4 - 5
1. Gastrointestinal Issues - Nausea, vomiting, and abdominal pain.
2. Fatigue and Weakness - General tiredness or lack of energy.
3. Weight Gain or Loss - Changes in weight can occur.
4. Dizziness - Some patients experience dizziness or lightheadedness.
5. Sleep Disturbances - Trouble sleeping or changes in sleep patterns.

Serious Side Effects (Require medical attention): 3 - 5
1. Severe Allergic Reactions - Rash, itching, swelling, severe dizziness, difficulty breathing.
2. Bone Density Loss - Prolonged use can lead to decreased bone density, increasing the risk of osteoporosis and fractures.
3. Cardiovascular Issues - Increased risk of heart attack, stroke, or other cardiovascular events.
4. Liver Function Changes - Signs include yellowing of the skin or eyes, dark urine.
5. Severe Mood Changes - Severe depression or suicidal thoughts.
6. Tumor Flare - Temporary worsening of symptoms in prostate cancer patients at the beginning of treatment.

Mechanism of Action:
Prostap works by initially stimulating and then profoundly suppressing the release of gonadotropins (luteinizing hormone (LH) and follicle-stimulating hormone (FSH)) from the pituitary gland. This suppression leads to decreased production of sex hormones (testosterone in men, estrogen in women), which can help control hormone-sensitive conditions such as prostate cancer and endometriosis.

Conclusion:
Prostap injections are a versatile treatment for various hormone-sensitive conditions in both men and women. While effective, they come with a range of potential side effects. It is essential for patients to discuss the benefits and risks with their healthcare

provider, undergo regular monitoring, and report any concerning symptoms to ensure the best possible outcome.

RADIOTHERAPY

Radiotherapy, also known as radiation therapy, is a medical treatment that uses high doses of radiation to kill cancer cells and shrink tumours. It is a highly targeted therapy aimed at specific areas of the body and is used for various types of cancer. Here's a detailed explanation of radiotherapy, including its mechanisms, types, planning, delivery, and potential side effects:

Mechanism of Radiotherapy

Radiotherapy works by damaging the DNA within cancer cells. The high-energy radiation disrupts the DNA molecules, preventing the cells from dividing and growing. Over time, the damaged cells die, and the body naturally eliminates them. Healthy cells can also be affected by radiation, but they have a better ability to repair themselves compared to cancer cells.

Types of Radiotherapy

There are two main types of radiotherapy: external beam radiation therapy (EBRT) and internal radiation therapy (brachytherapy).

External Beam Radiation Therapy (EBRT)

Mechanism - EBRT delivers radiation from a machine outside the body. The most common type of machine used is a linear accelerator, which generates high-energy X-rays or electrons.
Techniques
3D Conformal Radiation Therapy (3D-CRT) - Uses imaging techniques to shape the radiation beams to match the shape of the tumour.
Intensity-Modulated Radiation Therapy (IMRT) - Modulates the intensity of the radiation beams and shapes them precisely to the tumour.
Image-Guided Radiation Therapy (IGRT) - Uses imaging during treatment to improve precision.
Stereotactic Radio-surgery (SRS) and Stereotactic Body Radiotherapy (SBRT) - Deliver very high doses of radiation to

small, well-defined tumours in the brain (SRS) or body (SBRT) with extreme precision.

Internal Radiation Therapy (Brachytherapy)

Mechanism - Brachytherapy involves placing radioactive sources directly inside or near the tumour.

Types

Intracavitary Brachytherapy - Radioactive sources are placed in body cavities, such as the uterus or cervix.

Interstitial Brachytherapy - Radioactive sources are implanted directly into the tissue, such as in prostate cancer.

Planning and Delivery

Treatment Planning

Simulation - The planning process begins with a simulation, where the patient undergoes imaging studies such as CT scans, MRI, or PET scans to determine the exact location, shape, and size of the tumour.

Marking - The treatment area is marked on the skin or with temporary markers.

Treatment Plan - A team of specialists, including radiation oncologists, dosimetrists, and medical physicists, creates a detailed treatment plan. This plan specifies the type of radiation, dosage, and delivery schedule, aiming to maximise the dose to the tumour while minimising exposure to healthy tissues.

Delivery

Sessions - Radiotherapy is typically delivered in multiple sessions (fractions) over several weeks. Each session is brief, usually lasting only a few minutes, but the setup time can be longer.

Positioning - The patient is carefully positioned on a treatment table, and immobilisation devices may be used to ensure precision.

Administration - The radiation is delivered according to the treatment plan. The patient remains still, and the radiation beams are directed at the tumour from different angles.

Potential Side Effects

Radiotherapy can cause both acute and long-term side effects, which vary depending on the treatment area and dose.

Acute Side Effects I developed 2

1. Skin Reactions - Redness, irritation, and peeling in the treated area.

2. Fatigue - A common side effect that can last for weeks to months.

3. Local Symptoms - Depending on the treatment area, symptoms can include nausea, hair loss, and difficulty swallowing.

Long-Term Side Effects

1. Fibrosis - Scarring and stiffness in the treated tissues.

2. Secondary Cancers - A small risk of developing new cancers in the treated area years after treatment.

3. Organ-Specific Effects - Such as reduced lung function or heart issues if these areas were irradiated.

Follow-Up and Support

Regular follow-up appointments are essential to monitor the patient's response to treatment, manage side effects, and detect any recurrence of cancer. Supportive care, including nutritional support, physical therapy, and counselling, may be offered to help manage side effects and improve quality of life.

Radiotherapy is a cornerstone of modern cancer treatment, often used in combination with surgery, chemotherapy, and immunotherapy to achieve the best outcomes for patients. Its precision and effectiveness make it a vital tool in the fight against cancer.

RADIOTHERAPY FOR BREAST CANCER

Radiotherapy, also known as radiation therapy, is a common treatment for breast cancer that uses high-energy rays to target and destroy cancer cells. It can be used after surgery to eliminate any remaining cancer cells, reduce the risk of recurrence, or as a primary treatment in certain cases. Here's a detailed explanation of radiotherapy for breast cancer, including its side effects:

Types of Radiotherapy for Breast Cancer
External Beam Radiotherapy (EBRT)
The most common form of radiotherapy for breast cancer.
High-energy x-rays are directed at the breast from a machine outside the body. Treatment is usually given five days a week for several weeks.
Internal Radiotherapy (Brachytherapy)
Less common and typically used in specific cases.
Radioactive sources are placed inside the breast tissue near the cancer site. May be used as a boost along with EBRT or as an alternative in certain cases.

Process of Radiotherapy
Consultation and Planning
Initial consultation with a radiation oncologist to discuss the treatment plan. Planning session (simulation) involves imaging scans (CT, MRI) to map the area to be treated.
Marking the treatment area on the skin with small tattoos or semi-permanent ink.
Treatment Sessions
The patient lies on a treatment table in the same position each time.
The radiotherapy machine (linear accelerator) delivers precise doses of radiation to the targeted area.
Each session lasts a few minutes, but setup and positioning can take longer.
Post-Treatment Care
Regular follow-up appointments to monitor side effects and

assess the effectiveness of the treatment.

Side Effects of Radiotherapy
Radiotherapy for breast cancer can cause various side effects, which can be acute (short-term) or chronic (long-term).

Acute Side Effects 2 - 4
1. Skin Reactions - Redness, dryness, and itching in the treated area. Skin may become sore, similar to sunburn. Peeling or blistering in severe cases.

2. Fatigue - A common side effect that can persist for several weeks after treatment ends. May be mild to severe, affecting daily activities.

3. Breast Changes - Swelling and tenderness of the breast. Sensation of heaviness or tightness.

4. Pain and Discomfort - Mild to moderate pain in the treated area.
Can be managed with pain relievers and supportive care.

Chronic Side Effects
1. Skin Changes - Long-term changes in skin colour and texture.
Increased sensitivity or reduced sensation in the treated area.

2. Breast Tissue Changes - Permanent changes in size, shape, and firmness of the breast. Fibrosis (hardening) of breast tissue.

3. Lymphedema - Swelling of the arm or breast due to damage to the lymphatic system. More common if lymph nodes were also treated or removed.

4. Heart and Lung Effects - Risk of heart or lung damage, especially if the left breast is treated. Increased risk of heart disease and lung issues in rare cases.

5. Second Cancers - A very small risk of developing a secondary cancer in the treated area years later.

Managing Side Effects
Skin Care
Use mild soap and avoid harsh chemicals.

Keep the treated area clean and dry.

Wear loose-fitting clothing to reduce irritation.

Apply prescribed creams or ointments to soothe the skin.

Fatigue Management

Get plenty of rest and pace activities throughout the day.

Engage in light exercise, such as walking, to boost energy levels. Eat a balanced diet and stay hydrated.

Pain Relief

Over-the-counter pain medications like acetaminophen or ibuprofen. Consult with a doctor for stronger pain relief if necessary.

Lymphedema Prevention

Perform gentle exercises to improve lymphatic drainage.

Avoid heavy lifting and repetitive arm movements.

Wear compression garments if recommended by a healthcare provider.

Regular Monitoring

Regular check-ups with the oncology team to monitor and manage side effects. Report any new or worsening symptoms promptly.

Radiotherapy is a crucial component of breast cancer treatment, significantly reducing the risk of recurrence and improving survival rates. While side effects can be challenging, most are manageable with appropriate care and support.

REMOVING A SURGICAL DRAIN

Removing a surgical drain from the site of an operation is a medical procedure that should be performed by a healthcare professional to ensure it is done safely and to minimise the risk of infection or complications. However, here's a general overview of the process that healthcare professionals might follow:

Preparation Gather Supplies:
- Sterile gloves
- Sterile gauze pads
- Antiseptic solution
- Dressing supplies
- Scissors (if needed)
- Disposable container (for the removed drain)
- Tape or other securing materials for the new dressing

Patient Preparation:
- Explain the procedure to the patient to ensure they understand and are comfortable.
- Position the patient comfortably, ensuring easy access to the drain site.
- Ensure privacy and maintain a sterile field around the procedure area.

Procedure
Hand Hygiene:
- Wash hands thoroughly with soap and water, then dry them.
- Put on sterile gloves.
Inspect the Site:
- Check the drain site for signs of infection, such as redness, swelling, or unusual discharge.
- Assess the amount and type of fluid being drained to ensure it is appropriate for removal.

Clean the Area:
- Clean around the drain site with an antiseptic solution to minimise the risk of infection.

Remove Sutures (if present):
- If the drain is secured with sutures, carefully cut and remove them using sterile scissors and tweezers.

Clamp the Drain (if necessary):
- If the drain is still actively draining fluid, you may need to clamp it to prevent leakage during removal.

Remove the Drain:
- Gently and steadily pull the drain out in a continuous motion. The patient might feel some discomfort, but the process should not be painful.
- If resistance is encountered, stop and assess to ensure it is safe to proceed.

Inspect the Site:
- Once the drain is removed, inspect the site again for any signs of infection or other issues.

Apply Pressure:
- Apply gentle pressure to the site with a sterile gauze pad to control any bleeding.

Post-Removal Care

Clean the Site Again:
- Clean the site once more with an antiseptic solution.

Dress the Wound:
- Cover the site with a sterile dressing and secure it in place with tape or other appropriate materials.
- Provide instructions to the patient on how to care for the site, including signs of infection to watch for.

Dispose of the Drain:
- Dispose of the drain and any used materials in a proper biohazard container.

Document the Procedure:
- Document the removal process in the patient's medical record, noting the condition of the site, the amount and type of fluid drained, and any patient reactions.

Follow-Up

Monitor the Site:
- Instruct the patient to monitor the site for signs of infection or complications and to keep the area clean and dry.
Schedule Follow-Up:
- Schedule a follow-up appointment to ensure proper healing and to address any concerns the patient may have.

Important Notes
Sterility: Maintaining a sterile field is crucial to prevent infection.
Patient Comfort: Be gentle and communicate with the patient throughout the procedure to ensure their comfort and cooperation.
Professional Supervision: This procedure should only be performed by a qualified healthcare professional.

If you are not a healthcare professional, do not attempt to remove a surgical drain on your own. Always seek professional medical assistance.

SYMPHYSIS PUBIS DYSFUNCTION (SPD)

Symphysis Pubis Dysfunction (SPD) is a condition associated with pregnancy that causes pain and discomfort in the pelvic region. It occurs when the ligaments that normally keep the pelvic bone (specifically the symphysis pubis, a joint at the front of the pelvis) stable become overly relaxed and stretchy. This relaxation is often due to hormonal changes, particularly the hormone relaxin, which prepares the body for childbirth by loosening the ligaments.

Symptoms
Pain in the pelvic region: This can be sharp or dull and may radiate to the lower back, hips, groin, perineum, or thighs.
Discomfort when moving: Activities such as walking, climbing stairs, turning over in bed, or standing on one leg (e.g., while dressing) can exacerbate the pain.
Clicking or grinding sensation: Some individuals may feel or hear clicking or grinding in the pelvic area.
Limited mobility: Severe SPD can lead to difficulty in walking or performing daily activities.

Causes
Hormonal changes: The hormone relaxin causes the ligaments in the pelvic area to loosen in preparation for childbirth, but in some cases, this can lead to instability and pain.
Biomechanical factors: Changes in posture and gait during pregnancy can put additional stress on the pelvic joints.
Previous pelvic injury: A history of pelvic trauma or injury can increase the likelihood of developing SPD.

Diagnosis
Diagnosis is typically made based on a physical examination and the description of symptoms. In some cases, imaging studies such as ultrasound or MRI may be used to rule out other conditions or to assess the severity of the dysfunction.

Treatment

Physical therapy: Specialised exercises to strengthen the pelvic floor, abdominal muscles, and lower back can help stabilise the pelvic region.

Support belts: Pelvic support belts can provide external stability to the pelvic area and reduce pain.

Pain relief: Pain management options include acetaminophen, prescribed pain medications, or ice packs to reduce inflammation.

Lifestyle modifications: Avoiding activities that exacerbate pain, such as heavy lifting or standing on one leg, can help manage symptoms.

Manual therapy: Techniques such as chiropractic adjustments or osteopathic manipulations may provide relief.

Prognosis

SPD typically resolves after childbirth when hormone levels return to normal and the ligaments regain their pre-pregnancy tightness. However, some women may continue to experience symptoms for a few months postpartum, and in rare cases, the condition can persist longer.

Managing SPD effectively often requires a multidisciplinary approach, including medical professionals, physical therapists, and possibly chiropractors, to ensure both maternal comfort and safety during pregnancy.

WHITE COAT SYNDROME

White coat syndrome, also known as white coat hypertension, refers to a phenomenon where a patient's blood pressure readings are higher when measured in a medical setting, such as a doctor's office, compared to readings taken in other settings, like at home. This can be attributed to anxiety or nervousness experienced during medical appointments, often due to the presence of healthcare professionals wearing white coats, hence the name.

Here are some key points about white coat syndrome:

Anxiety-Induced The elevated blood pressure is thought to result from the anxiety some people feel during a medical visit. The stress of being in a clinical environment can cause a temporary increase in blood pressure.

Diagnosis To diagnose white coat hypertension, doctors may compare blood pressure readings taken in the office with those taken at home or with a 24-hour ambulatory blood pressure monitor. If the readings are consistently higher in the medical setting but normal elsewhere, white coat syndrome may be the cause.

Health Implications While white coat syndrome itself might not be harmful, it can complicate the diagnosis and management of hypertension (high blood pressure). Over time, frequent episodes of high blood pressure can still pose risks to cardiovascular health.

Management To manage this condition, healthcare providers might recommend regular home blood pressure monitoring to get a more accurate picture of a patient's typical blood pressure levels. Relaxation techniques and stress management strategies can also help reduce anxiety during medical visits.

Prevalence It is estimated that about 20-30% of patients with elevated blood pressure readings in a clinical setting experience white coat hypertension. It is more common among individuals who have higher levels of anxiety or who are particularly nervous about medical procedures.

Understanding and addressing white coat syndrome is crucial for accurate blood pressure measurement and effective hypertension management.

WIRE GUIDE PROCEDURE

The wire guide procedure, also known as wire localisation or needle localisation, is a preoperative technique used to precisely mark the location of a tumour, usually in the breast, before surgical removal. This procedure is particularly important for tumours that are not palpable (cannot be felt) and are only visible on imaging studies. Here's a detailed description of what is involved and the reasons for having this procedure:

Procedure Steps
Imaging Guidance:
The procedure is typically performed using imaging techniques such as mammography, ultrasound, or MRI to accurately visualise the tumour.
Local Anaesthesia:
The area where the wire will be inserted is numbed with local anaesthesia to minimise discomfort.
Insertion of the Guide Wire:
A thin, hollow needle is inserted through the skin and guided to the tumour using the imaging technique.
Once the needle is in the correct position, a fine wire with a hook or barb on the end is threaded through the needle and into the tumour.
The hook secures the wire in place within the tumour.
Needle Removal:
The needle is then removed, leaving the wire in place. The end of the wire protrudes from the skin, and this is taped down to prevent movement.
Confirmation:
Additional imaging may be performed to ensure the wire is correctly positioned.

Reasons for the Procedure
Precise Tumour Localisation: For tumours that are not palpable, it is crucial to mark their exact location to aid the surgeon in removing the correct tissue. The wire acts as a guide to ensure that the surgeon can locate and excise the tumour

with accuracy.

Minimising Healthy Tissue Removal: Accurate localisation helps the surgeon remove the tumour with clear margins (adequate surrounding healthy tissue), reducing the likelihood of leaving cancerous cells behind. This precision minimises the removal of healthy tissue, preserving more of the breast.

Improving Surgical Outcomes: By providing a clear target, wire localisation helps to reduce the risk of needing additional surgeries. Clear and accurate excision of the tumour in the first surgery improves overall surgical outcomes and patient satisfaction.

Assisting Pathological Examination: The wire helps pathologists by marking the area of concern, making it easier to examine and confirm the removal of the entire tumour during postoperative analysis.

Context and Applications

Breast Cancer: Wire localisation is most commonly used for non-palpable breast tumours detected through screening mammography.

Other Tumours: It can also be applied to tumours in other parts of the body that are difficult to locate by touch or visual inspection during surgery.

Alternatives

Radioactive Seed Localisation: Involves placing a tiny radioactive seed in the tumour instead of a wire, which can be detected during surgery using a special probe.

Magnetic Seed Localisation: Uses a small magnetic seed to localise the tumour, detected during surgery with a magnetic probe.

In summary, wire guide procedures are a critical component of the preoperative planning for tumour excision surgeries, particularly for non-palpable tumours, enhancing the accuracy of tumour removal and preserving as much healthy tissue as possible.

Printed in Great Britain
by Amazon